IBIZAN HOUND

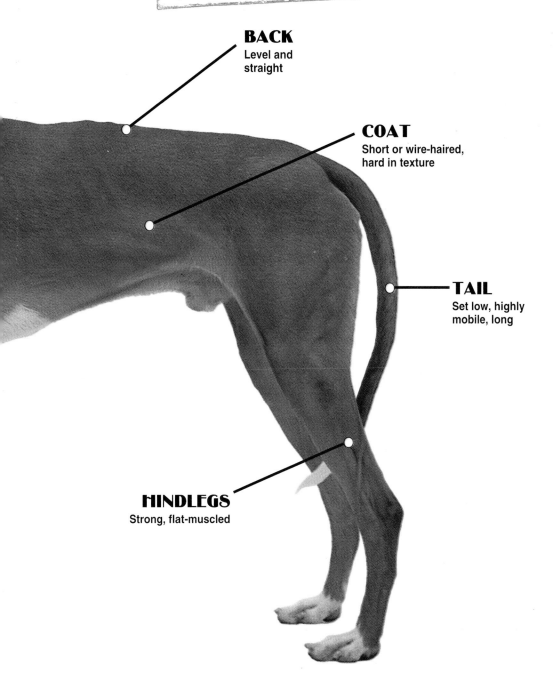

BACK
Level and
straight

COAT
Short or wire-haired,
hard in texture

TAIL
Set low, highly
mobile, long

HINDLEGS
Strong, flat-muscled

Title page: Ibizan Hound photographed by Annemiek Hawkins.

Photographers: Nicole Biloski, Grant Carter, Steve Donnaby, Isabelle Francais, Annemiek Hawkins, Carol Kaufman, Kohler Photography, Alanna Lowry, Leslie Lucas, Marge Morris, Mariette Murphy, John O'Malley, Judy Parker, Michelle Paulin, Robert Pearcy, Lisa Puskas, Ron Reagan, Alex Smith, Nancy Stabler, Mary Toliver, Peter Viveiros

Distributed in the UNITED STATES to the Pet Trade by T.F.H. Publications, Inc., 1 TFH Plaza, Neptune City, NJ 07753; on the Internet at www.tfh.com; in CANADA by Rolf C. Hagen Inc., 3225 Sartelon St., Montreal, Quebec H4R 1E8; Pet Trade by H & L Pet Supplies Inc., 27 Kingston Crescent, Kitchener, Ontario N2B 2T6; in ENGLAND by T.F.H. Publications, PO Box 74, Havant PO9 5TT; in AUSTRALIA AND THE SOUTH PACIFIC by T.F.H. (Australia), Pty. Ltd., Box 149, Brookvale 2100 N.S.W., Australia; in NEW ZEALAND by Brooklands Aquarium Ltd., 5 McGiven Drive, New Plymouth, RD1 New Zealand; in SOUTH AFRICA by Rolf C. Hagen S.A. (PTY.) LTD., P.O. Box 201199, Durban North 4016, South Africa; in JAPAN by T.F.H. Publications. Published by T.F.H. Publications, Inc.

MANUFACTURED IN THE
UNITED STATES OF AMERICA
BY T.F.H. PUBLICATIONS, INC.

IBIZAN HOUND

A COMPLETE AND RELIABLE HANDBOOK

Lisa Puskas

RX-144

CONTENTS

INTRODUCTION TO THE IBIZAN HOUND

The first time I looked into the regal, amber eyes of an Ibizan Hound I was completely captivated. Although I was familiar with many hound breeds, this particular hound was unique. As I stared, intrigued with this animal that at first glance looked so deerlike and refined, I noticed the sunlight glistening over her strong, smooth muscles—the muscles of a hunter. She looked directly into my eyes, her head held proudly. Her body was solidly poised, with ears alert, and I sensed that I was being instantly yet thoroughly examined by this modern-day Anubis. With simply a

A rare and elegant breed, the unique Ibizan Hound is a tolerant and remarkably devoted companion.

glance, this rare hound had obtained the upper hand and she knew it. A healthy dose of respect was added to my curiosity.

Momentarily, her look softened and those deep pools of amber eyes beckoned me to come nearer. "I know I am beautiful and clearly in control, yet I enjoy your attention," they seemed to say. As I approached, she raised herself onto her hind legs and delicately placed one front paw into each of my hands. She was as light and graceful as a prima ballerina. She gently moved her head toward my face, then softly rubbed her muzzle on my cheek. My heart melted.

"What type of hound is she?" I asked her owner. "She is an Ibizan Hound," he answered, " a breed that can trace its ancestry back to the ancient Egyptians." "And her name?" I inquired. "Charisma," he stated. "Of course," I said to myself, "What other name could so befit royalty?"

That first meeting was in 1974. I was eventually married to Charisma's owner and had the privilege of owning her, or as I am sure Charisma would say, she owned me. Since that time, I have never been without one of these lovely hounds and I cannot imagine myself without one in the future. A part of my life changed forever on that day.

Over the years, each of the Ibizan Hounds that I have shared my heart and home with have been different in many ways. However, they all share a common trait that will always endear me to this breed. There is not a more tolerant or remarkably devoted love than that bestowed on an owner by the elegant, beautiful, and unique Ibizan Hound. The humans that receive this love feel very special indeed.

Am. Ch. Ishtar Charisma, owned by Lisa Puskas.

HISTORY OF THE IBIZAN HOUND

Sighthound-type dogs were depicted as early as 10,000 BC in paintings discovered on the walls of an ancient Spanish cave. These dogs are called sighthounds because they hunt mainly by sight. They existed throughout the Mediterranean region and are considered by many to be the earliest known ancestors of several of today's sighthound breeds, including the Podenco Ibicenco, or Ibizan Hound.

FROM EGYPT

Ancient Egyptian stone carvings, drawings, and statues show a dog with large, prick ears and a lithe body; features that strikingly resemble the present-day

It is not known how the ancestors of the Ibizan Hound originally came to Egypt, but the dogs remained there for thousands of years. A statue found in the tomb of King Tut, called "The Ancient Watchdog of the Dead," bears a close resemblance to the present-day Ibizan.

It is believed that Phoenician sailors in the eighth century brought the Ibizan Hound to the island of Ibiza. Centuries of Spanish breeding produced Can. Ch. Muerdago F.Ch. Owners: Susan and Peter Viveiros.

Ibizan Hound. It is uncertain how these dogs originally came to Egypt, but it is certain that they remained there for thousands of years. Early artwork, dating from about 3,000 BC, shows the dogs hunting large, gazelle-like game. Perhaps the most famous image is the statue of Anubis, the *Watchdog of the Dead*, found in the tomb of King Tut and believed to have been carved around 1,360 BC. When this statue was originally discovered, it was believed to be the image of a jackal. However, as the Ibizan Hound gained in popularity, people noticed the uncanny resemblance that Anubis bears to the present-day Ibizan Hound. Around 50 BC, even Cleopatra owned a dog that closely resembles the Ibizan.

In 1958, Egypt obtained several Ibizan Hounds in an effort to reintroduce the breed to its ancestral home.

TO IBIZA

It is believed that Phoenician sailors in the eighth century brought these dogs to the island of Ibiza, one of the Balearic Islands located off of the coast of Spain in the Mediterranean Sea. The Balearic Islands consist of several islands, including Mallorca (the largest), Menorca, and Ibiza. On Ibiza, these dogs survived by hunting small game, mainly rabbits. The farmers living on the island depended on the breed not only to keep rabbits from eating their crops, but also to deliver a rabbit dinner for the farmer's family, as life was hard and food was not always plentiful. Only the fittest dogs survived, which further shaped the breed into master hunters. On Ibiza, the Ibizan Hound remained true to type.

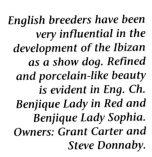

English breeders have been very influential in the development of the Ibizan as a show dog. Refined and porcelain-like beauty is evident in Eng. Ch. Benjique Lady in Red and Benjique Lady Sophia. Owners: Grant Carter and Steve Donnaby.

Although labeled as a sighthound, the Ibizan is a three-way hunter, using his keen senses of sight, scent, and sound to hunt game. These senses were honed by thousands of years of living on the island of Ibiza. It is a thrilling sight to see an Ibizan Hound hunting in the field, using his powerful and high jumping ability to clear tall brush with ease. The breed is seemingly tireless and can sustain an effortless, flowing trot, the gait that they use to track and flush game, for long stretches of time. On the islands, much linebreeding and inbreeding occurred, setting the breed's type and characteristics firmly into the limited gene pool. Remarkably, the dogs were known as a very healthy, hearty breed.

From Ibiza, the breed spread to many parts of the world. The legendary Hannibal, who lived on Ibiza, was reputed to have taken some of these hounds with him on his famous journey across the Alps. Today, the Ibizan can be found in many parts of the world.

THE SPANISH MAINLAND

The Spanish mainland has been referred to as the "land of the rabbits." Dogs thrived in this environment. On Mallorca, La Marquesa de Belgida of Barcelona established a kennel and was a great friend to the Ibizan Hound. She enjoyed showing her dogs on the Spanish mainland. From the Spanish breed ring, she introduced the Ibizan to conformation shows in other parts of Europe. Her most famous dogs, Ch. Guindoa de Jamma-Nura and Ch. Kento can be found in the pedigrees of some of today's Ibizan Hounds. On the Spanish mainland today, the breed hunts over natural, brush-filled terrain, just as they would have hunted hundreds of years ago. Here, the Ibizan Hound functions more as a hunting breed than it does in many other parts of the world.

TO ENGLAND

English breeders have been very influential in the development of the Ibizan Hound as a show dog, and the breed has enjoyed much success. A long quarantine period that was placed on imported dogs from many other countries made it difficult to import new bloodlines. As has often happened with the Ibizan Hound, the gene pool remained small, and much linebreeding took place within the limited breeding stock available. Through the years, many of the established kennels produced dogs with characteristics that were quite distinctive, not only to their kennel, but also to England. Lovely, refined, porcelain-like beauty is evident in many of the English Ibizan Hounds. Leo The Brave stands out as perhaps the most influential sire of the breed in England. His name appears in the pedigrees of most English Ibizan Hounds and many English champions are linebred on him. One of his most successful breedings was to his granddaughter, Divels Licha. This mating produced one of the most famous of the exported English dogs, International and Mexican Ch. Eridu Maestro of Loki. There were 28 Ibizans registered with The Kennel Club in 1998 and 35 entries for the breed at Crufts in 1999.

IN THE UNITED STATES

The first Ibizan Hounds imported to the US were Hannibal and Certera, imported from Ibiza in 1956 by Colonel and Mrs. Seoane. Mrs. Seoane loved Ibiza and wrote beautiful poetry about the Ibizan Hound and her visits to the island. The Seoanes bred and promoted the dogs in the US, and together they founded the first Ibizan Hound club in the country. The breed grew slowly in number and popularity.

Although the first Ibizan Hounds were imported from Ibiza, the hounds that were imported from England actually make up the largest part of the Ibizan Hound gene pool in the US. The English import Int./Mex. Ch. Eridu Maestro of Loki, or "Maya," certainly left his mark on this country.

Maya traveled to dog shows throughout the US with his owner, Mr. Richard Edwards. At the time, the Ibizan Hound was in the American Kennel Club (AKC) miscellaneous class. Mr. Edwards and Maya became true ambassadors for the breed throughout the country. A stunning white dog, Maya attracted attention wherever he went; however, it was his warm and gentle personality that won him and the breed loyal followers. Maya sired several litters, and he proved to be quite dominant at bestowing his wonderful qualities to his offspring. He stood out among other stud dogs as *the* foundation sire of the breed in the US.

In the US, the Ibizan Hound is kept mainly as a family companion and show dog. Throughout the 1980s, the breed's gene pool remained quite limited. In an effort to add new bloodlines to their breeding stock, many US breeders began importing dogs from other countries. Ultimately, most of the dogs in the US, even many of the newly imported dogs, can eventually trace their ancestry back to the same English or Spanish ancestors. Thus far, this has not proven itself to be a problem for the Ibizan Hound.

THROUGHOUT THE WORLD

Ibizan Hounds are now commonly being imported and exported between countries—Canada, England, Finland, Holland, Norway, South Africa, and more. Ibizan history has traditionally been a tale of strategic isolation, which has kept the breed quite pure and true to type. With the modern blending of bloodlines throughout the world, the future result will be a more homogenous blend of the distinct breed types and gene pools that have developed to date.

Representing many generations of American breeding, Am/Can. Ch. Paradise Legacy O'Bramblewood sired #1 and Best in Show winning offspring in three countries. Owner: Lisa Puskas.

CHARACTERISTICS OF THE IBIZAN HOUND

The Ibizan Hound is a strong, swift hunter whose primary quarry is rabbits. Unlike many dog breeds that have been bred by man to serve certain purposes, nature had the ultimate hand in forming the Ibizan Hound. Seemingly tireless while hunting, the Ibizan can sustain his light, smooth trot for hours. After sighting his prey, he is capable of quick bursts of speed, allowing him to run down even the fastest game. During the chase, he is unequaled in his agility around and over obstacles in the field.

TEMPERAMENT

The Ibizan Hound's playful, puppy-like nature makes him seem quite clown-like at times. Ibizans make

Unequaled in his agility, the Ibizan Hound is a strong, swift hunter capable of quick bursts of speed that allow him to run down even the fastest game.

A wonderful and loving family pet, the typical Ibizan is sensitive, accepts training readily, and is easily housebroken.

wonderful family pets, as they are especially loving, loyal, and devoted to their owners. The typical Ibizan is sensitive, accepts training readily, and is easily housebroken.

Most Ibizan Hounds have very stable temperaments and are bold yet curious and sometimes slightly reserved around strangers. Some Ibizans exhibit behavior typical to many sighthounds, namely an aloofness or wariness around strangers; however, this should never be confused with shyness or fearfulness, which would be a temperament fault. Aggressiveness, except when guarding home and family, and extreme shyness are not typical to this breed and are highly undesirable behaviors.

DESCRIPTION OF IBIZAN HOUND FORM

Man should never attempt to change the Ibizan Hound to suit some current trend or fashion in the conformation ring, as so often happens. It is important that breeders and judges alike understand that the Ibizan Hound has always been a dog of function, not fashion. This breed is a piece of history and breeders have a responsibility to preserve the Ibizan Hound in his original form for future generations. Understanding the purpose of each of the parts that make up the Ibizan and how each of these parts so perfectly performs the job that it was intended to do is primary to the preservation of the breed.

Type

The Ibizan Hound is strong yet refined, extreme in his abilities yet moderately built. Ibizan type (the certain qualities or look that sets this breed apart from the rest) is definitely distinct to this breed.

The huge, high-set ears are one of the most unusual qualities of the breed. These ears, which catch even the tiniest sounds, serve the Ibizan Hound well while hunting in the field. They are the exception to the otherwise moderate look of this hound.

Much of the Ibizan's elegance comes from his long, graceful legs and smooth, flat muscle. The Ibizan Hound possesses clean, fine bone, which means that the bone should never be thick or heavy in appearance. This fine bone is deceptively strong. Likewise, the strong yet flat muscles called for in this breed

Much of the Ibizan Hound's elegance comes from his long, graceful legs, smooth muscle, and fine bone.

The Ibizan's huge, high-set ears are one of the breed's most unusual qualities. Able to detect the tiniest of sounds, they serve him well while hunting in the field.

should never be rounded or bulging. Heavy bone and muscle add extra weight, and an Ibizan carrying this added weight would soon tire in the field.

Size

The height of the Ibizan Hound has steadily increased in recent years due, in part, to better care and nutrition, but also to the erroneous notion that bigger is better and more easily noticed in the conformation ring. Many breeders have shown and bred only the tallest dogs in their litters, selling their smaller counterparts as pets. It must be remembered that the historic function of this breed has been as a hound that hunts rabbits, not as a show dog. Oftentimes, some of the smallest dogs in a litter prove to be the best in the field. The Ibizan Hound has always been a hound of moderate size, and this quality should be appreciated in the show ring.

Head

People constantly refer to the Ibizan look as "deer-like." In addition to the hound's elegant, graceful body, his large, high-set ears and finely chiseled facial features certainly contribute to this impression. However, unlike the deer, the Ibizan Hound has many qualities indicative of a hunter.

One of these qualities, the Ibizan jaw, is well suited to catching and retrieving game. It is long with strong teeth perfectly opposed in a scissors bite. The skull of the Ibizan Hound is long and flat. One of the most important points of correct head type is that the skull and the muzzle, when viewed in profile, are on parallel planes. The head is referred to as dry-fleshed, which means free from wrinkles and folds.

The light pigment of the eyes and nose is particularly striking. The small, oblique eye is of an amber or caramel color, which affords a regal look. The nose is of a rosy, flesh color, and solid or butterfly (partially pigmented) noses are equally acceptable. The nose blends well with the color of the body.

Topline

Many people share an incorrect view of exactly what part of a dog makes up his topline. The correct definition of a topline is the dog's upper profile, from ears to tail. The Ibizan Hound topline is smooth and flowing. The long neck has a slight arch and flows into withers that are of moderate width.

The back refers to the part of the topline that begins at the end of the withers. The withers attach to a straight, level back, with the exception that the loin area is slightly arched and the croup is slightly sloping, which makes the tail set rather low.

Forequarters

The front assembly of the Ibizan Hound is unique to the breed. The shoulder is well laid back and joins to an upright or straight upper arm. This front assembly places the deepest part of the chest behind the elbow. It is imperative that the Ibizan has this angulation, because it is what allows the breed to be unsurpassed in maneuverability and quick turning ability when running after its prey. The muscling is strong and on a properly constructed hound, the elbows will be held close to the body when moving, never appearing loose or sloppy.

Hindquarters

The strong muscling in the hindquarters is smooth,

flat, and distinctly different from the round-muscled appearance of a Greyhound. The rear is moderately angulated and provides moderate drive (the rear thrust that propels a dog forward) when moving.

Balance

Balance is the symmetry of a dog's separate parts in relationship to each other. In the Ibizan Hound, this is what separates the average Ibizans from the great Ibizans, and it is oftentimes elusive.

The Ibizan Hound should be one to two inches longer than he is tall. The correct way to measure the body length of the Ibizan is to measure the distance from the foremost point of the shoulder to the rearmost projection of the upper thigh or buttocks. Often, the Ibizan is measured from the withers, not the point of the shoulder, which is incorrect. Height is measured from the highest point of the withers to the ground while the dog is stacked in a show pose.

Balanced Movement

As the Ibizan Hound lifts his front leg and flexes his wrist, the rear must deliver the proper thrust needed to propel the dog forward. Excessive rear angulation delivers too much forward motion, which creates a flat, far-reaching front stride that lacks proper lift. The opposite of this is a dog lacking in rear angulation, which cannot supply the needed forward movement. The dog will not cover ground smoothly and efficiently, and his movement will appear choppy. The correct movement at the trot is a light, single tracking gait (the imprints of the paws appear as a single line of travel under the body). The Ibizan will lift his front leg, almost horizontally, smoothly extend his wrist, then gracefully (never pounding) return it to the ground. The movement is efficient, covers ground, and should never appear to hackney (the exaggerated high lift of the front legs that restricts forward movement). An Ibizan Hound with superior movement will appear to skim effortlessly over the ground.

Coat

There are two types of coat in the Ibizan Hound: wire-haired and short (often called smooth). Short-coated dogs possess hair that is no longer than about an inch in length. Wire-haired Ibizans can have hair from one inch to about three inches in length, with generous areas of hair on the face,

back, thighs, and tail. When these two types of Ibizans are bred together, both wire and smooth pups can appear in the same litter. Often, the type of wire coat that results from these matings is relatively short, with some longer hair on the face, back, and other parts of the body (often called a broken coat). Most of these dogs are registered as wire-haired and can produce full wire-haired puppies when bred to a wire-haired mate. Aside from the coat description, the AKC breed standard for both the wire-haired and short-coated Ibizan Hounds is the same.

There are two types of coat in the Ibizan Hound: short (often called smooth) and wire-haired. The wire-haired Ibizan can have hair from one to three inches in length.

Both wire-haired and short-coated Ibizans are efficient hunters, alone or in a pack. On Ibiza, the hounds developed as a hunter of small game. There the Ibizan Hound did not need the heavier body type of a hunter that brings down large quarry, so both varieties remained fine-boned, agile, and swift. The breed became such accomplished hunters that a pack of Ibizans could efficiently bring down the deer that inhabit the Spanish mainland.

Color

The only acceptable colors for the Ibizan Hound are white and red, either solid or in any combination. Some dogs are a light, yellowish-red, resembling a lion's color, while others are closer to an Irish Setter-type red. Many are almost totally white or red. No color or pattern should be preferred when judging this breed.

STANDARD FOR THE IBIZAN HOUND

AMERICAN KENNEL CLUB STANDARD

General Appearance—The Ibizan's clean-cut lines, large prick ears and light pigment give it a unique appearance. A hunting dog whose quarry is primarily rabbits, this ancient hound was bred for thousands of years with function being of prime importance. Lithe and racy, the Ibizan possesses a deer-like elegance combined with the power of a hunter. Strong, without appearing heavily muscled, the Ibizan is a hound of moderation. With the exception of the ears, he should not appear extreme or exaggerated.

Possessing a deer-like elegance combined with power, the Ibizan's clean-cut lines, large prick ears, and light pigment give him a unique appearance. This is nine-month-old Bramblewoods In The Know, CGC. Owner: Alanna Lowry.

In the field the Ibizan is as fast as top coursing breeds and without equal in agility, high jumping, and broad jumping ability. He is able to spring to great heights from a standstill.

Proportion, Size, and Substance—*Size*—The height of dogs is 23+ inches to 27+ inches at the withers. Bitches are 22+ inches to 26 inches at the withers. There is no preference for size within this range. Sizes slightly over or under the norms are not to be regarded as demerits when other qualities are good. *Weight*—Average weight of dogs is 50 pounds; bitches, 45 pounds. *Proportion*—Slightly longer than tall. *Substance*—The Ibizan possesses clean, fine bone. The muscling is strong, yet flat, with no sign of heaviness.

Head—Long and narrow in the form of a sharp cone truncated at its base. Finely chiseled and extremely dry fleshed.

Expression—The Ibizan has an elegant, deer-like look. The *eyes* are oblique and small, ranging in color from clear amber to caramel. The rims are the color of the nose and are fully or partially pigmented. The appearance of the eye is intelligent, alert, and inquisitive. The *ears* are large, pointed, and natural. On alert, the ear should never droop, bend, or crease. Highly mobile, the ear can point forward, sideways, or be folded backward, according to mood. On alert, the lowest point of the base is at the level of the eye. On frontal examination, the height of the ear is approximately 2+ times that of the widest point of the base.

Skull—Long and flat, prominent occipital bone, little defined *stop*; narrow brow. The *muzzle* is elongated, fine, and slender with a very slight Roman convex. The length of the eyes to point of nose is equal to the distance from eyes to occiput. The muzzle and skull are on parallel *planes*. The *nose* is prominent, extending beyond the lower jaw. It is of a rosy flesh color, never black or liver, and tends to harmonize with that of the coat. Pigment is solid or butterfly. Nostrils are open. *Lips* are thin and tight and the color of the nose. Flews are tight and dry fleshed. *Bite*—The teeth are perfectly opposed in a scissors bite, strong and well set.

Neck, Topline, Body—The *neck* is long, slender, slightly arched, and strong, yet flat muscled. The *topline*, from ears to tail, is smooth and flowing. The *back* is level and straight. *Body*—The chest is deep and long with the breastbone sharply angled and prominent. The ribs are slightly sprung. The brisket is approximately 2+ inches above the elbow. The deepest part of the chest, behind the elbow, is nearly to, or to, the elbow. The abdomen is well tucked up but not exaggerated. The **loin** is very slightly arched, of medium breadth, and well muscled. The **croup** is very slightly sloping. The **tail** is set low, highly mobile, and reaches at least to the hock. It is carried in a sickle, ring, or saber position, according to the mood and individual specimen.

Forequarters—Angulation is moderate. The **shoulders** are elastic but never loose with moderate breadth at the withers. The shoulder blades are well laid back. At the **point of the shoulder** they join to a rather upright **upper arm**. The **elbow** is positioned in front of the deepest part of the chest. It is well held in but not so much as to restrict movement. **Legs**—The forearms are very long, strong, straight, and close, lying flat on the chest and continuing in a straight line to the ground. Bone is clean and fine. The **pasterns** are strong and flexible, slightly sloping, with well developed tendons. **Dewclaw** removal is optional. **Feet:** hare-foot. The toes are long, closed and very strong. Interdigital spaces are well protected by hair. Pads are durable. Nails are white.

Hindquarters—Angulation is moderate with the hindquarters being set under the body. **Legs**—The thighs are very strong with flat muscling. The hocks are straight when viewed from the rear. Bone is clean and fine. There are no rear dewclaws. The **feet** are as in front.

The only acceptable colors for the Ibizan Hound are white and red, either solid or in combination. Nor/ Sw/Eng. Ch. Puljon Pink Panther. Owners: Grant Carter, Steve Donnaby, and Rosenhill Kennel.

Coat—There are two types of coat; both untrimmed. *Short*—shortest on head and ears and longest at back of the thighs and under the tail. *Wire-haired* can be from one to three inches in length with a possible generous moustache. There is more hair on the back, back of thighs, and tail. Both types of coat are hard in texture and neither coat is preferable to the other.

Color—White or red (from light, yellowish-red called "lion" to deep red), solid or in any combination. No color or pattern is preferable to the other. *Disqualify* any color other than white or red.

Gait—An efficient, light, and graceful single-tracking movement. A suspended trot with joint flexion when viewed from the side. The Ibizan exhibits smooth reach in front with balanced rear drive, giving the appearance of skimming over the ground.

Temperament—The Ibizan Hound is even-tempered, affectionate, and loyal. Extremely versatile and trainable, he makes an excellent family pet, and is well suited to the breed ring, obedience, tracking, and lure-coursing. He exhibits a keen, natural, hunting instinct with much determination and stamina in the field.

Disqualification—Any color other than white or red.
Approved September 11, 1989
Effective November 1, 1989

Extremely versatile and trainable, the Ibizan is well suited to the conformation ring, obedience, tracking, and lure coursing. Am. Ch. Hemato's J-Mark Star Maiden. Owner: Jeff Macek.

YOUR PUPPY'S NEW HOME

Before actually collecting your puppy, it is better to purchase the basic items you will need in advance of the pup's arrival date. This allows you more opportunity to shop around and ensure that you have exactly what you want, rather than having to buy a lesser quality product in a hurry. Ask the breeder what food the puppy is eating and have a supply on hand before the puppy arrives.

It is always better to collect the puppy as early in the day as possible. In most instances, this will mean that the puppy has a few hours with your family before it is time to retire for his first night's sleep away from his former home. Ask the breeder to supply you with a toy or cloth that has been with the puppy's mother and littermates. When placed in the puppy's new sleeping area, the familiar smell can be comforting.

Before your Ibizan puppy arrives at his new home, be sure to purchase the basic items he'll need and have a supply of the food he's been eating on hand.

When collecting your puppy for the trip home, bring a crate with you. It will provide your Ibizan with a safe place to lie down and rest while traveling, both now and as he grows into adulthood. This six-month-old pup is raring to go.

Be sure to advise the breeder at what time you hope to arrive for the puppy, as this will obviously influence the feeding of the pup that morning or afternoon. If you arrive early in the day, then they will likely only give the pup a light breakfast so as to reduce the risk of travel sickness. Be sure to bring some paper towels to clean up any unexpected accidents.

At the time that you collect your puppy, the breeder should supply you with his shot and worming record. It is very important that the puppy is given his shots when they are due, and it is preferable that he has at least two vaccinations before being placed in a new environment. You should always take your new puppy to a veterinarian for a health check as soon as possible, even if he appears to be healthy. There are many health problems that can only be diagnosed with a thorough health check. Many breeders provide a health guarantee of 72 hours or so and will take the puppy back and refund the purchase price if a veterinarian pronounces the puppy unhealthy. If such a guarantee is offered, be sure to obtain it in writing.

If the puppy is to be registered with the AKC, the breeder should supply you with his registration papers and a pedigree at the time you take him home. Some breeders may ask you to sign a contract stipulating such things as the spaying or neutering of your dog, sole or co-ownership, or even the type of care that you will provide for your dog. Read any contract carefully and do not sign it unless you understand it and agree to the terms listed.

When collecting your puppy for the trip home, you should bring a travel crate with you. The crate will provide your pup with a safe place to lie down and rest while traveling in the car. If it is a long trip, the puppy will no doubt wish to relieve his bowels, so you will have to make a few stops. On a long journey you may need a rest yourself and can take the opportunity to let the puppy get some fresh air. Be sure he is supervised and kept on a leash at all times when he is in a public place. However, do not let the puppy walk where there may have been a lot of other dogs, because he might pick up an infection. Also, if he relieves his bowels at such a time, do not just leave the feces where they were dropped. This is the height of irresponsibility. It has resulted in many public parks and other places actually banning dogs. You can purchase poop-scoops from your pet shop and should have them with you whenever you are taking the dog out where he might relieve himself in a public place.

Your journey home should be made as quickly as possible. If it is a hot day, be sure the car interior is amply supplied with fresh air. It should never be too hot or too cold for the puppy. The pup must never be placed where he might be subjected to a draft. If the journey requires an overnight stop at a motel, be aware that other guests will not appreciate a puppy crying half the night. You must regard the puppy as a baby and comfort him so he does not cry for long periods. The worst thing you can do is to shout at him or smack him. This will scare your puppy and get your relationship off to a bad start. You wouldn't smack a baby, and your puppy is still very much just that.

Oftentimes, Ibizan puppies are shipped quite some distance to their new home by airplane. Your puppy will have spent many hours in his crate when he finally reaches his destination. He will probably need to relieve his bowels and should be offered fresh water and a light snack before his car trip home.

ON ARRIVING HOME

By the time you arrive home, the puppy may be very tired, in which case he should be taken to his sleeping area and allowed to rest. Children should not be allowed to interfere with the pup when he is sleeping. If the pup is not tired, he can be allowed to investigate his new home but always under your close supervision. After a short look around, the puppy will no doubt appreciate a light meal and a drink of water. Do not overfeed him at his first meal, because he will be in an excited state and more likely to be sick.

Although it is an obvious temptation, you should not invite friends and neighbors around to see the new arrival until he has had at least 48 hours in which to settle down. Indeed, if you can delay this longer then do so, especially if the puppy is not fully vaccinated. At the very least, the visitors might introduce some bacteria on their clothing that the puppy is not immune to. This aspect is always a risk when a pup has been moved to a new home, so the fewer people the pup meets in the first week, the better.

DANGERS IN THE HOME

Your home holds many potential dangers for a little mischievous puppy, so you must think about these in advance and be sure he is protected from them. The more obvious are as follows.

Open Fires

A mesh screen guard should protect all open fires, so that there is no danger of the pup being burned by spitting pieces of coal or wood.

Although it's tempting, do not introduce your puppy to friends and neighbors for at least 48 hours, especially if he's not fully vaccinated. He needs time to adjust to his new environment and to build up his immunities.

Be sure to puppy-proof your home to keep your curious Ibizan pup from harm. Bunker, owned by Mariette Murphy.

Electrical Wires

Puppies just love chewing on things so be sure that all electrical appliances are neatly hidden from view and are not left plugged in when not in use. It is not sufficient simply to turn the plug switch to the off position; pull the plug from the socket.

Open Doors

A door would seem a pretty innocuous object, yet with a strong draft it could kill or injure a puppy easily if it is slammed shut. Always ensure that there is no risk of this happening. It is most likely to occur during warm weather when you have windows or outside doors open and a sudden gust of wind blows through.

Balconies

If you live in a high-rise building, obviously the pup must be protected from falling. Be sure he cannot get through any railings on your patio, balcony, or deck.

Ponds and Pools

A garden pond or a swimming pool is a very danger-ous place for a little puppy to be near. Be sure it is well screened so there is no risk of the pup falling in. It takes barely a minute for a pup, or a child, to drown.

The Kitchen

While many puppies will be kept in the kitchen, at least while they are toddlers and not able to control their bowel movements, this is a room full of danger, especially while you are cooking. When cooking, keep the puppy in an exercise pen or in another room where he is safely out of harm's way. Alternatively, if you have a crate, put him in it so he can still see you but is well protected.

Washing Machines

When using washing machines, be aware that more than one puppy has clambered in to have a nap and received a wash instead! If you leave the washing machine or clothes dryer door open and leave the room for any reason, be sure to check inside the machine before you close the door and switch it on.

Small Children

Toddlers and small children should never be left unsupervised with puppies. In spite of such advice, it is amazing just how many people not only do this, but also allow children to pull and maul young pups. They should be taught from the outset that a puppy is not a plaything to be dragged about the home, and they should be promptly scolded if they disobey.

Children must be shown how to safely lift a young puppy. Failure to correctly educate children about dogs could result in the child being hurt one day. When a puppy is lifted, his weight must always be supported. To lift the pup, first place one hand under his chest. Next, secure the pup by using your other hand to hold his neck. Now you can lift him and bring him close to your chest. Never lift a pup by his ears, and while he can be lifted by the scruff of his neck where the fur is loose, this should never be done.

Chewing

Ibizan Hound puppies love to chew. Watch your puppy carefully while he is loose in the house and keep poisonous plants and toxic objects out of reach. Have many appropriate puppy chew toys available at all times. If you do not, your puppy may chew your rugs, furniture, or even your kitchen cabinets.

Beyond the dangers already cited, you may be able to think of other ones that are specific to your home, such as steep basement steps or the like. Go around your home and check out all potential problems. You'll be glad you did!

THE FIRST NIGHT

The first few nights a puppy spends away from his

mother and littermates are quite traumatic for him. He will feel very lonely or maybe cold and will certainly miss the heartbeat of his siblings when sleeping. To assist him in overcoming his loneliness, it may help to place a clock that makes a loud ticking sound next to his bed. This will in some way soothe him, as the clock ticks to a rhythm not dissimilar from a heartbeat. A cuddly toy or an object with the scent of his mother and littermates on it, obtained from the puppy's breeder, may also help in the first few nights. A dim nightlight may provide some comfort to the puppy, because his eyes will not yet be fully able to see in the dark. The puppy may want to leave his bed for a drink or to relieve himself.

If the pup does whimper in the night, there are two things you should not do. One is to get up and chastise him, because he will not understand why you are shouting at him. The other is to rush to comfort him every time he cries, because he will quickly realize that if he wants you to come running, all he needs to do is to holler loud enough!

By all means give your puppy some extra attention on his first night, but afterward quickly refrain from doing so. The pup will cry for a while but then settle down and go to sleep. Of course, some pups are worse than others in this respect, so you must use balanced judgment in the matter. Many owners take

Ask your breeder to supply you with a toy or cloth that has been with your Ibizan's mother or littermates. The familiar smell will be comforting to him when placed in his new sleeping area.

If you have other pets in the home, your Ibizan puppy should be introduced to them under careful supervision. This lucky pup gets a hug from his new housemate.

their pups to bed with them. However, you should only do this if you intend to let this be a permanent arrangement, otherwise it is hardly fair to the puppy. Remember that a grown Ibizan Hound can weigh around 50 pounds. If you have decided to have two puppies, then they will keep each other company and you will have fewer problems.

OTHER PETS

If you have other pets in the home, then the puppy must be introduced to them under careful supervision. Puppies will get along with many other pets, but you must make due allowance for the respective sizes of the pets concerned and appreciate that your puppy has a rather playful nature. Due to the hunting nature of this breed, it would be very foolish to leave your Ibizan pup with a bird or a rabbit, as he might bite the smaller animal and get altogether too rough with it. Small kittens may not be able to sufficiently defend themselves against a large Ibizan Hound puppy. An adult cat could obviously give the pup a very bad scratch, though generally cats will jump clear of pups and watch them from a suitable vantage point. Many adult Ibizan Hounds live peacefully or become great friends with other small animals, but some Ibizans always consider them as game to chase—always be very careful.

HOUSETRAINING

Undoubtedly, the first form of training your puppy will undergo is in respect to his toilet habits. To achieve this, you can use either newspaper or scented housebreaking pads that are available at many pet supply stores. The Ibizan Hound is usually fairly easy to housebreak; however, a puppy cannot control his bowels until he is a few months old and not fully until he is an adult. Therefore, you must anticipate his needs and be prepared for a few accidents. The prime times a pup will urinate and defecate are shortly after he wakes up from a sleep, shortly after he has eaten, and after he has been playing awhile. He will usually whimper and start sniffing the ground, searching the room for a suitable place. You must quickly pick him up and place him on the newspaper or pad. Hold him in position gently but firmly. He might leave without doing anything on the first one or two occasions, but if you simply repeat the procedure every time you think he wants to relieve himself, then eventually he will get the message.

When he does defecate as required, give him plenty of praise, telling him what a good puppy he is. The pad or newspaper must, of course, be replaced after each use. Puppies do not like using a dirty toilet any more than you do. The pup's toilet can be placed near the door, and as he gets older, it can be placed outside while the door is open. The pup will then start to use it while he is outside. From that time on, it is easy to get the pup to use a given area of the yard.

Make sure you take your puppy outside to relieve himself after eating, sleeping, and playing. Praise and positive reinforcement are an important part of the housebreaking process.

Crate Training

Many breeders recommend the popular alternative of crate training. Upon bringing the pup home, introduce him to his crate. The crate should be placed in a restricted, draft-free area of the home. Put the pup's Nylabones® and other favorite toys in the crate, along with a wool blanket or other suitable bedding. As the puppy matures and can control his bowels, his natural cleanliness instincts will prohibit him from soiling in the place where he sleeps, namely his crate. A crate that is approximately three feet long by two and one-half feet tall is the size that will be necessary for an adult Ibizan Hound. A puppy can use a smaller crate, but make sure to adjust the size of the crate as the puppy grows. Do not put a dog into a crate that is too small for him. The dog should be able to stand and turn around comfortably. Whenever the pup is taken out of his crate, he should be brought outside (or to his newspaper or pad) to do his business. Never use the crate as a place of punishment. You will see how quickly your pup takes to his crate, considering it as his own safe haven from the big world around him.

Do not leave your Ibizan Hound puppy in his crate for extended periods of time during the day. The crate should be used mainly for sleeping. Ideally, the puppy

Crate training is the easiest and fastest way to housetrain your Ibizan puppy. His natural instincts will prohibit him from soiling the place where he sleeps.

should be allowed to go in and out of the open crate during the day. If you work all day and are considering leaving your puppy in his crate while you are gone—don't. Other arrangements should be made, as it is not fair to the poor puppy to leave him crated night and day. Too much time spent in the crate without enough exercise can cause poor growth and stiff, sore movement in your puppy. One solution would be to purchase an exercise pen that will confine the puppy while allowing him room to walk around. Make sure that it is tall enough to keep your growing pup from escaping over the top.

THE EARLY DAYS

You will, no doubt, be given much advice on how to bring up your puppy. This will come from dog-owning friends, from neighbors, and through articles and books you may read on the subject. Some of the advice will be sound and some will be nothing short of rubbish. What you should do, above all else, is to keep an open mind and let common sense prevail over prejudice and worn-out ideas. There is no one way that is superior to all others, just as there is no one dog that is an exact replica

Extremely versatile and trainable, the Ibizan makes an excellent family pet—he is even-tempered, affectionate, and loyal.

of another. Each is an individual and must be regarded as such.

A dog never becomes disobedient, unruly, or a menace to society without the full consent of his owner. Your puppy may have many limitations, but in so many instances, the singular biggest limitation he is confronted with is his owner's inability to understand his needs and how to cope with them.

Remember to never be harsh when training your Ibizan Hound puppy. They are a sensitive breed and train easily with kindness. The Ibizan Hound wants to please and responds readily to a loving voice and touch.

IDENTIFICATION

It is a sad reflection on our society that the number of dogs and cats stolen every year runs into many thousands. To these can be added the number that get lost. If you do not want your cherished pet to be lost or stolen, then you should see that he is carrying a permanent identification number, as well as an identification tag on his collar.

Permanent markings come in the form of tattoos placed on the inner side of a pup's upper rear leg. The number given is then recorded with one of the national registration companies. Research laboratories will not purchase dogs carrying numbers because they realize that these are clearly someone's pets and not abandoned animals. As a result, thieves will normally abandon dogs so marked and this at least gives the dog a chance to be taken to the dog pound where the number can be traced and the dog reunited with his family. At this time, the only problem with this method is that there are a number of registration bodies, so unless your dog is wearing a tag with the name and phone number of the organization it is registered with, it is not always apparent which one to call. However, each registration body is aware of his competitors and will normally be happy to supply their phone numbers and addresses. Those holding the dog can check out which one you are with.

Another permanent form of identification is the microchip, a computer chip that is no bigger than a grain of rice that is injected between the dog's shoulder blades. The dog feels no discomfort. The dog also receives a tag that says he is microchipped. If the dog is lost and picked up by the humane society, they can trace the owner by scanning the microchip. Microchips are usually highly reliable; however, humane societies have reported that microchips have occasionally migrated from the point of injection. This can make the microchip harder to locate when scanning.

Although a permanent form of identification is strongly recommended, it is also important that your dog always wear a collar and tag along with any other form of identification. A tag takes the form of a metal or plastic disk large enough for you to place your dog's name, your phone number, and your address on it.

In virtually all places in America, you will be required to obtain a license for your puppy. This may not become applicable until the pup is six months old, but it might apply regardless of his age. Much depends upon the state within a country or the country itself, so check with your veterinarian if the breeder has not already advised you on this.

In many cities, phone systems and websites are becoming available to aid in the recovery of lost pets. If someone has lost or found a pet, they can call a phone number or access a website that will allow them to enter a description of the animal and its location into the system. The information that they enter will be instantly available to anyone else who calls, and the systems can quickly match lost pets to their owners.

If your Ibizan is lost, a collar with an identification tag can aid in his safe return.

LIVING WITH AN IBIZAN HOUND

Life with an Ibizan Hound is never boring. Although he is no longer on the island of Ibiza chasing rabbits, your Ibizan is quite adept at entertaining himself in other ways. His antics are often amusing, but you must be one step ahead of him or your sweet little Ibizan puppy will soon seem like a whirling tornado.

Ibizan puppies are quite active and require room to run and play. A safe, outdoor play area is a must for

Ibizan puppies are quite active and require room to run and explore. A safe, fenced-in outdoor exercise area is a must.

Playfulness is an integral part of what makes up the Ibizan personality. These rambunctious five-month-old pups are well suited to playing with each other, but should be closely supervised when around small children until they are mature adults.

the energetic, inquisitive youngster. Puppies cannot be expected to respond consistently to your commands. Just as you would childproof your home, you must puppy-proof any areas to which your puppy has access.

A strong, six-foot-high fence is a must for your Ibizan Hound. A three-foot-high exercise pen may contain a small puppy; however, by six months of age, that same puppy will have grown to almost his full height. Once an Ibizan puppy sets his mind to going over, under, or around something, he can be very determined. A strong, six-foot fence is important, because when the puppy realizes that he is securely contained, his thoughts of escaping will diminish and he will turn his attention elsewhere.

Puppies require lots of room to run and play in order to grow strong and healthy. If you cannot provide room for your pup to run or you are away from home most of the day and must leave your pup crated, think twice before obtaining a young puppy.

PLAYFUL PERSONALITY

Ibizan Hounds seem to retain their puppy-like playfulness well into old age. Playfulness is an integral part of what makes up the Ibizan's personality, and it is very important to this breed.

From the time Ibizan pups can walk, they spend most of their waking moments immersed in play. Young pups use their mouth to latch onto each other's neck, legs, or tail and wrestle until one pup, quite vocally, cries that he has had enough of the game. At a few months of age, pups delight in playing games of tag. This is serious business, as they are perfecting the skills that they would use to hunt game in the wild.

An Ibizan pup will crouch down, similar to a cat in a stalking position, and slowly and silently inch forward, one step at a time. Concentrating intently, every muscle tensed, the pup will suddenly spring forward and jump on his prey, which is usually his unsuspecting playmate. The playmate seems to thoroughly enjoy this, quickly turning, dodging, and running away from his pretend attacker. Puppies never try to actually hurt each other during this game, and the roles of attacker and prey are continually reversed.

Hunting behavior can also be seen if you play fetch with your puppy. Show your puppy a small toy made for dogs, such as a rope toy or stuffed animal. When your puppy acts interested in it, throw it a short distance and watch your puppy run after it and pounce on it. Often, your puppy will pick it up with his mouth and shake it thoroughly. In the field, your Ibizan would use this same shaking action to disable any small prey it might catch.

Young Ibizan puppies are well suited to playing with each other but are entirely too rough in their play with very small children. Toddlers and young children can mistakenly and easily be knocked down or scratched by a rambunctious Ibizan Hound puppy that simply does not know his own strength. Close supervision is necessary until the puppy is older, when he will be very trustworthy and careful around children.

The adult Ibizan enjoys playtime just as much as his youthful counterparts. Although he enjoys playing with other dogs, he especially enjoys playtime with his owner. When in a playful mood, the Ibizan will often stand in front of his owner and quickly lower his front legs to the ground, his hindquarters remaining in a standing position and his tail wagging wildly. This is the Ibizan signal that he has chosen you to be his playmate. Your Ibizan delights in showing off his skills to you. Clap your hands and he will take off, running swift circles around you so that you can admire his quickness. Throw him a ball or Frisbee, and he will jump high to catch it.

If you are too busy to play at the moment, your hound may gently take your arm in his mouth and tug on it, begging you to play a game of tag. Many Ibizan Hounds teasingly snap their teeth together in a playful though harmless menace.

The Ibizan Hound definitely knows the difference between real hunting and playing. As strong and swift as adult Ibizans can be, they are amazingly kind and gentle. Adult Ibizan Hounds are exceptionally tolerant and loving around children and make excellent pets.

DEVOTED COMPANION

Ibizan Hounds are very social animals. They desire and inherently need companionship. The Ibizan is most content when he is a part of a family, a position for which he is well suited.

Ibizans make wonderful companions. They are very loyal and affectionate. Often, an Ibizan will bond more closely to one particular family member. They may follow this person from room to room throughout the house, quietly curling up in a corner just to be near them.

Once an Ibizan Hound makes you his own, he is dedicated to you for life. His foremost desire will be to please you, and he will lovingly obey your commands. This bond develops from mutual love, respect, and trust. The sensitive Ibizan will never trust or respect someone who treats him harshly. This gentle hound will withdraw, become depressed, and fail to respond to commands if treated improperly.

Loving human companionship is necessary to the Ibizan Hound's well-being. Very social animals, the Ibizan is most content when he is part of a family.

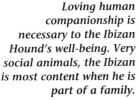

Loving human companionship is important to the Ibizan Hound, and he will not like to be left alone for long periods of time. If you must leave your Ibizan

alone during the day, it would be wise to have a playmate for him. Having another dog to play with will help to keep him physically fit and prevent him from becoming lonely.

AS A WATCHDOG
As a whole, the breed is very protective of their home and family. The Ibizan has a deep bark that would make any intruder take notice. I have owned some Ibizans that would, I am sure, quickly bite an unwelcome intruder. Others would simply bark, stand their ground, and not approach the intruder unless directly confronted. One particular male Ibizan that I owned never met a stranger that he did not like. I am sure that he would have gladly tried to befriend any intruder—not the usual Ibizan reaction.

Each Ibizan definitely has his own distinct personality. Many times a puppy learns to bark and protect the home from watching the protective response of an older dog. If the older dog is friendly toward strangers, the puppy most likely will learn to react in the same manner.

CLIMATE CONCERNS
The island of Ibiza, where the Ibizan Hound developed, has a very temperate climate to which the Ibizan Hound is well suited. Care must be taken if your Ibizan will be living in a climate with extremes in temperatures.

The Ibizan should not be left outside for long periods of time in very cold weather. His coat is not suited to providing much protection from the cold, and he will be most uncomfortable. Even if you buy a dog sweater to keep your Ibizan Hound warm, his thin ears could easily be frostbitten in severe weather and much care should be taken.

Although the Ibizan is more adaptable to a warmer climate, he should not be left outside if the temperature is too warm. A good rule to follow is that if you feel uncomfortably warm outside, your Ibizan will probably feel the same. Continuous panting is a sign that your Ibizan is too warm. It is important to always have fresh water and shade available outdoors during warm weather.

On the island of Ibiza, Ibizan Hounds are known to dig huge underground tunnels capable of holding several dogs. These tunnels keep the dogs cool and out of the hot sun during the summer months. More than one unsuspecting Ibizan owner has left their hounds in their yard, only to return to find their dogs happily resting in one of these quickly and efficiently dug tunnels.

ADOPTING AN IBIZAN

The Ibizan Hound is very adaptable to new surroundings. Most people who have adopted an adult Ibizan have had few, if any, problems adjusting the dog to his new home. Because they enjoy human companionship so much, adopted dogs usually bond easily to a new owner.

A national registry such as the American Kennel Club can provide you with the names and phone numbers of persons to contact concerning the adoption or rescue of an Ibizan.

THE OLDER DOG

Sometime at around ten years of age, your Ibizan's activity levels and needs will change. He will still enjoy playing with you or his canine companions; however, he will tire more easily and need more rest. It is important to make sure that your hound has comfortable bedding in which to sleep. Maintaining proper weight for your less active dog is equally important, which may mean lower levels of fat and protein in his diet.

Have your older Ibizan checked by a veterinarian yearly to help him stay healthy. Detecting age-related problems early can lead to a longer, more comfortable life for your pet.

Have your older Ibizan Hound checked by your veterinarian yearly to help him stay healthy. If your vet discovers and treats an age-related problem early, it may lead to a longer, more comfortable life for your pet.

FEEDING YOUR IBIZAN HOUND

Dog owners today are fortunate that they live in an age when considerable cash has been invested in the study of canine nutritional requirements. This means that dog food manufacturers are very concerned about ensuring that their foods are of the best quality. The result of all their studies, apart from the food itself, is that dog owners are bombarded with advertisements telling them why they must purchase a given brand. The number of products available to you is unlimited, so it is hardly surprising to find that dogs in general suffer from obesity and an excess of vitamins, rather than the reverse. Be sure to feed age-appropriate food designed to meet the nutritional needs of your puppy, adult, or senior dog. Generally, breeders

For the first few weeks of life, a baby Ibizan's mother supplies all of the nutrition he requires. These two-week-old pups will need to be fed numerous times throughout the day.

Always be sure to feed age-appropriate food designed to meet the nutritional needs of your puppy, adult, or senior dog.

recommend dry food supplemented by canned if needed.

FACTORS AFFECTING NUTRITIONAL NEEDS

Activity Level: A dog that lives in a country environment and is able to exercise for long periods of the day will need more food than the same breed of dog living in an apartment and given little exercise.

Quality of the Food: Obviously, the quality of food will affect the quantity required by a puppy. If the nutritional content of a food is low, the puppy will need more of it than if a better quality food was fed.

Balance of Nutrients and Vitamins: Feeding a puppy the correct balance of nutrients is not easy, because the average person is not able to measure out ratios of one to another, so it is a case of trying to see that nothing is in excess. However, only product testing or your veterinarian can be the source of reliable advice.

Genetic and Biological Variation: Apart from all of the other considerations, it should be remembered that each puppy is an individual. His genetic make-up will influence not only his physical characteristics, but also his metabolic efficiency. This being so, two pups from the same litter can vary quite a bit in the amount of food they need to perform the same function under the same conditions. If you consider the potential combinations of all of these factors, you will see that pups of a given breed could vary quite a bit in the amount of food they will need. Before discussing feeding quantities, it is valuable to know at least a little about the composition of food and its role in the body.

COMPOSITION AND ROLE OF FOOD

The main ingredients of food are protein, fats, and carbohydrates, each of which is needed in relatively large quantities when compared to the other needs of vitamins and minerals. The other vital ingredient of food is, of course, water. Although all foods obviously contain some of the basic ingredients needed for an animal to survive, they do not all contain the ingredients in the needed ratios or type. For example, there are many forms of protein, just as there are many types of carbohydrates. Both of these compounds are found in meat and in vegetable matter, but not all of those that are needed will be in one particular meat or vegetable. Plants do not contain certain amino acids that are required for the synthesis of certain proteins needed by dogs.

Likewise, vitamins are found in meats and vegetable matter, but vegetables are a richer source of most. Meat contains very little carbohydrates. Some vitamins can be synthesized by the dog, so they do not need to be supplied via the food. Dogs are omnivores, which means their digestive tract has evolved to need a high quantity of meat as compared to humans. The digestive system of omnivores is unable to break down the tough cellulose walls of plant matter, but it is easily able to assimilate proteins from meat.

In order to gain its needed vegetable matter in a form that it can cope with, the omnivore eats all of its prey. This includes the partly digested food within the stomach. In commercially prepared foods, the cellulose is broken down by cooking. During this process, the vitamin content is either greatly reduced or lost altogether. Therefore, the manufacturer adds vitamins once the heat process has been completed. This is why commercial foods are so useful as part of a feeding regimen, providing they are of good quality and from a company that has prepared the foods very carefully.

Proteins

These are made from amino acids, of which at least ten are essential if a puppy is to maintain healthy growth. Proteins provide the building blocks for the puppy's body. The richest sources are meat, fish, and poultry, together with their by-products. The latter will include milk, cheese, yogurt, fishmeat, and eggs. Vegetable matter that has a high protein content includes soybeans, together with numerous corns and other plant extracts that have been dehydrated. The actual protein content needed in the diet will be determined both by the activity level of the dog and his age. The total amount of protein needed will also be influenced by the digestibility factor of the food given.

Fats

These serve numerous roles in the puppy's body. They provide insulation against the cold and help buffer the organs from knocks and general activity shocks. They provide the richest source of energy and reserves of this, and they are vital in the transport of vitamins and other nutrients, via the blood, to all other organs. Finally, it is the fat content within a diet that gives it palatability. It is important that the fat content of a diet should not be excessive. This is because the high-energy content of fats (more than twice that of protein or carbohydrate) will increase the overall energy content of the diet. The puppy will adjust his food intake to that of his energy needs, which are obviously more easily met in a high-energy diet. This will mean that while the fats are providing the energy needs of the puppy, the overall diet may not be providing his protein, vitamin, and mineral needs, so signs of protein deficiency will become apparent. Rich sources of fats are meat, their by-products (butter and milk), and vegetable oils such as safflower, olive, corn, or soy bean.

The amount of exercise your Ibizan receives affects his food intake. A very active dog will require more food to eat than a less active dog of the same size.

Carbohydrates

These are the principal energy compounds given to puppies and adult dogs. Their inclusion within most commercial brand dog foods is for cost, rather than dietary needs. These compounds are more commonly known as sugars, and they are seen in simple or complex compounds of carbon, hydrogen, and oxygen. One of the simple sugars is called glucose, and it is vital to many metabolic processes. When large chains of glucose are created, they form compound sugars. One of these is called glycogen, and it is found in the cells of animals. Another, called starch, is the material that is found in the cells of plants.

Vitamins

These are not foods as such, but chemical compounds that assist in all aspects of an animal's life. They help in so many ways that to attempt to describe these effectively would require a chapter in itself. Fruits are a rich source of vitamins, as is the liver of most animals. Many vitamins are unstable and easily destroyed by light, heat, moisture, or rancidity. An excess of vitamins, especially A and D, has been proven to be very harmful. It is most unlikely there will be a deficiency provided that a puppy is receiving a balanced diet, whereas hypervitaminosis (an excess of vitamins) has become quite common due to owners and breeders feeding unneeded supplements. The only time you should feed extra vitamins to your puppy is if your veterinarian advises you to do so.

Minerals

These provide strength to bone and cell tissue, as well as assist in many metabolic processes. Examples are calcium, phosphorous, copper, iron, magnesium, selenium, potassium, zinc, and sodium. The recommended amount of all minerals in the diet has not been fully established. Calcium and phosphorous are known to be important in the diet, especially to puppies. They help in forming strong bone. As with vitamins, a mineral deficiency is most unlikely in pups given a good and varied diet.

Some breeders recommend the use of supplements to help the young Ibizan Hound's ears come up without folds or creases. Excess minerals can create bone, joint, and other problems, so it is especially important to check with your veterinarian before adding extra minerals to your dog's diet.

Your Ibizan should have a healthy, well-balanced diet that includes the proper amount of proteins, fats, and carbohydrates.

Water

This is the most important of all nutrients, as is easily shown by the fact that the adult dog is made up of about 60 percent water; the puppy contains an even higher percentage. Dogs must retain a water balance, which means that the total intake should be balanced by the total output. The intake comes either by direct input (the tap or its equivalent), plus water released when food is oxidized, known as metabolic water. Remember that all foods contain the elements hydrogen and oxygen that recombine in the body to create water. A dog without adequate water will lose condition more rapidly than one depleted of food, a fact common to most animal species.

AMOUNT TO FEED

The best way to determine dietary requirements is by observing the puppy's general health and physical appearance. If he is well covered with flesh, shows good bone development and muscle, and is an active, alert puppy, then his diet is fine. A puppy will consume about twice as much as an adult of the same breed. You should ask the breeder of your puppy to show you the amounts fed to their pups, as this will be a good starting point.

The puppy should eat his meal in about five to seven minutes. Any leftover food can be discarded or placed into the refrigerator until the next meal. Be sure that the food is fully thawed if your fridge is very cold. Some puppies prefer to have their food slightly warmed.

When serving dry food, make sure that the pieces are small enough so that a young puppy with a tender mouth can chew them. With a young pup, it is preferable to

The best way to determine your dog's dietary requirements is to observe his general health and physical appearance—if your Ibizan is well covered with flesh and shows good bone development and muscle, then his diet is fine.

moisten dry food with a little water and mix in a teaspoon or so of canned food. Puppies get excited over the scent of meat and this encourages them to make the transition from mother's milk to commercially prepared dry food. Many Ibizan Hound owners continue this practice throughout adulthood to encourage finicky eaters.

If the puppy quickly devours his meal and is clearly still hungry, then you are not giving him enough food. If he eats readily but then begins to pick at it or walks away leaving a quantity, then you are probably giving him too much food. Adjust the amount at the next meal, and you will quickly begin to appreciate what the correct amount is. If over a number of weeks the pup starts to look fat, then he is obviously overeating; the reverse is true if he starts to look thin.

On an Ibizan Hound, it is normal to see the last couple of ribs under the skin; however, if many ribs are clearly visible, the dog is too thin. Occasionally, some Ibizan Hounds remain too thin no matter how carefully their owners feed them. If your veterinarian has pronounced your thin dog to be otherwise healthy, there may be little that you can do to increase his weight. Do not add large amounts of human food to his diet, thinking it will help him to gain weight. You will simply have a spoiled hound on an unbalanced diet. With time, your dog will most likely reach his desired weight on his own as he matures.

WHEN TO FEED

It really does not matter what times of the day the puppy is fed, as long as he receives the necessary quantity of food. Fresh water should be available throughout the day. Puppies from weaning to 12 or 16 weeks of age need 3 or 4 meals a day. Older puppies and adult dogs should be fed twice a day. What is most important is that the feeding times are reasonably regular. They can be tailored to fit in with your own timetable; for example, 7 a.m. and 6 p.m. The dog will then expect his meals at these times each day. Keeping regular feeding times and feeding set amounts will help you monitor your puppy's or dog's health. If a dog that's normally enthusiastic about mealtimes and eats readily suddenly shows a lack of interest in food, you'll know something's not right.

FOOD ALLERGIES

Some Ibizan Hound owners have found it necessary to change their dog's diet because of food allergies. This type of allergy can show up in many forms, including a skin rash and diarrhea. To avoid this, certain foods may have to be omitted. Always check with your veterinarian if you suspect this problem. If you do change your dog's diet, it is important to do so slowly. Mix the old food and new food together for several days to give your dog's digestive system time to adjust. The Ibizan Hound is very sensitive to dietary changes. The sudden introduction of new foods will often cause diarrhea.

Some Ibizans, although not allergic to certain foods, have problems digesting them. This results in loose stools. While most Ibizan Hounds thrive on most any good-quality dog food, some Ibizans have problems digesting foods containing certain meats or grains. Speak to your vet if you suspect such a problem. With the many varieties of dog food available, the simple omission of certain ingredients from your dog's diet should be easy.

Establishing a feeding schedule with set amounts of food will help you to monitor your Ibizan's overall health.

GROOMING YOUR IBIZAN HOUND

If you have ever spent many hours grooming a Cocker Spaniel or other long-coated breed, you will appreciate the comparatively little effort needed to groom the Ibizan Hound. The Ibizan is a clean animal and bathes himself by licking himself all over, similar to a cat. In spite of his efforts, there are still some grooming procedures that you will need to perform. The main concerns when grooming this breed are keeping the coat and skin clean and healthy, making sure that the ears are free from dirt and debris, and trimming the nails.

Compared to other breeds, little effort is required to groom the Ibizan Hound. Unlike her long-coated friend, this hound requires only occasional brushing and no trimming. Int/Am. Ch. Henmar's Jemms Cactus Jewel. Owner: Marge Morris.

Ibizans do not usually have a problem with ear infections because of the constant air circulation a large, erect ear affords. However, regular cleaning should be part of your routine.

CLEANING THE SKIN AND COAT

Puppies may be afraid of the feel and sound of running water the first couple of times that they are bathed. To make these first, impressionable baths a positive experience, follow a few basic steps.

Always bathe your puppy in a warm place and use warm—never hot or cold—water. Place a nylon collar on the puppy so that you have something other than a wet, squirmy puppy to hold on to and place him in the tub where he is to be bathed. Have a bucket of warm water available nearby. Dip a washcloth into the bucket and use it to slowly wet your puppy, starting with the feet and working upward. Do the puppy's head last. Squeeze some mild dog shampoo onto your hands and gently massage it all over the puppy. Your puppy should enjoy his shampoo massage. To keep the puppy from shaking and spraying water and shampoo all over, gently hold his muzzle when he starts to shake. Talk to him and tell him what a good puppy he is. Be sure to carefully avoid his eyes and nose, as this would be most uncomfortable for the poor puppy and would surely implant in his mind a negative association with bath time. If the puppy is especially squirmy, you may want to avoid applying shampoo to the head area altogether.

After your puppy's shampoo is complete, place some warm water into a non-breakable cup and carefully pour the water over him until he is thoroughly rinsed. Any shampoo residue left in your puppy's coat may irritate his skin, so be sure to remove all traces of shampoo. Your puppy may not like the feel of water being poured over his face (and you certainly do not want to get water in his ears) so use a wet rag to remove all traces of shampoo from his head.

Thoroughly dry your puppy with a towel. If it is cold and your puppy will tolerate it, you might finish drying him with a blow dryer set on low, being careful that the air is not too hot for his tender skin. If it is a warm day, you may want to wash your puppy outside and let him air dry. Once he is dry, brush your puppy's coat with a soft, natural bristle brush. To maintain his coat, brushing him twice a week should be enough to remove any loose hairs.

EAR CARE

You would expect that the Ibizan Hound's large, erect ears would accumulate a lot of dirt and debris, yet they actually remain remarkably clean. The exception might be the older Ibizan, whose ears seem to accumulate more of a waxy buildup due to age. Fortunately, Ibizans usually do not have a problem with bacteria and fungi infections because of the constant air circulation that an erect ear affords.

To clean the ear, dampen a cotton ball with a mild soap and water solution and gently swab only the visible part of the inner side of the ear flap. Never prod deeply into the ear—to do so may cause damage. A cotton swab may be used to aid in the removal of dirt and debris from areas that are visible. Always be gentle, because the inside of the ear flap is sensitive and will bleed easily. To remove dirt that accumulates deeper in the ear, use a liquid ear wash recommended by your veterinarian and always follow label directions carefully.

NAIL TRIMMING

Because an Ibizan Hound's nails are white, the quick (the pink part of the nail that carries the blood

Begin grooming your dog at an early age—it will help him become accustomed to the weekly procedure. This well-behaved Ibizan is comfortable having his nails trimmed.

supply) is easy to see and avoid. The most difficult part of nail trimming is keeping the puppy still. It is always advantageous to have someone helping you the first few times you trim your puppy's nails. The puppy may be as good as gold during the first nail trimming session, only to balk wholeheartedly the next time.

Most nail trimmers sold at pet supply stores will work on a puppy, but when your puppy is grown, be sure to buy a nail trimmer made specifically for large dogs. With an assistant holding the puppy, have the puppy sit. Lift one paw and hold it firmly yet gently in your hand. Be prepared for your puppy to pull his paw back once he realizes what is going on. Clip just past the quick and by all means do not cut into it, as it will bleed and cause the puppy pain. Always have some styptic powder, which can be purchased from a pet supply store, on hand to stop the bleeding if you happen to cut into the quick by mistake. If in doubt about how close to the quick to cut, leave more nail rather than less.

How often the nails will need trimming will depend on many factors: genetics, the type of flooring the dog walks on, how much of the nail is removed when trimmed, etc. However, it is wise to go through the nail trimming routine weekly with a young puppy, even if you do not actually remove any part of the nail, so that he becomes accustomed to this procedure. Trimming the nails of an unruly adult can be very difficult.

TRAINING YOUR IBIZAN HOUND

Once your puppy has settled into your home and responds to his name, you can begin his basic training. Before giving advice on how you should go about doing this, two important points should be made. You should train the puppy in isolation of any potential distractions, and you should keep all lessons very short. It is essential that you have the full attention of your puppy. This is not possible if there are other people about, if there are televisions and radios on, or if there are other pets in the vicinity. Even when the pup has become a young adult, the maximum time

You can begin basic training once your new puppy has settled into your home and responds to his name.

Do not allow your Ibizan off-leash until he reliably responds to your commands—for his safety and the safety of others.

you should allocate to a lesson is about 20 minutes. However, you can give the puppy more than one lesson a day, three being as many as are recommended, each well spaced apart.

Before beginning a lesson, always play a little game with the puppy so he is in an active state of mind and thus more receptive to the matter at hand. Likewise, always end a lesson with fun time for the pup, and always (this is most important) end on a high note, praising the puppy. Let the lesson end when the pup has done as you require so that he receives lots of praise. This will really build his confidence.

Something that will greatly ease training is the use of food as a reward. An Ibizan Hound will do almost anything for his favorite food treat. He will quickly learn to associate the reward with his correct response to your commands and will eagerly perform to obtain a treat.

COLLAR AND LEASH TRAINING

Training a puppy to his collar and leash is very easy. Place a collar on the puppy, and although he will initially try to bite at it, he will soon forget it, the more so if you play with him. You can leave the collar on for a few hours. Some people leave their dog's collar with an identification tag on all of the time, which is a good idea. Others put a collar on the dog only when they are taking him outside. If the collar is to be left on, purchase a narrow one so it does not mark the fur.

Once the puppy ignores his collar, then you can attach the leash to it and let the puppy pull this along behind him for a few minutes. However, if the pup starts to chew at the leash, simply hold the leash but keep it slack, and let the pup go where he wants. The idea is to let him get the feel of the leash, but not get in the habit of chewing it. Repeat this for two days a couple of times a day, and the pup will get used to the leash without thinking that it will restrain him.

Next, you can let the pup understand that the leash will restrict his movements. The first time he realizes this, he will pull and buck or just sit down. Immediately call the pup to you and make a fuss over him. Never tug on the leash so the puppy is dragged along the floor, because this simply implants a negative thought in his mind.

If your puppy is particularly stubborn about walking on a leash, hold a small piece of a favorite food treat just out of reach and let him walk to it. Give him a little bite and repeat this in short training sessions. Soon your puppy will be walking on a leash without the aid of treats.

THE COME COMMAND

Come is the most vital of all commands, especially for the independent-minded dog. To teach the puppy to come, let him reach the end of a long lead then give the command and his name, gently pulling him toward

To teach your Ibizan to come, let him reach the end of a long lead and then give him the command as you say his name and gently pull him toward you. Am/Can. Ch. Luxor's Shout to the Top. Owners: Leslie Lucas and Glen Brand.

The sit is the foundation command for everything else your dog will learn. This Ibizan performs a perfect sit to please his companion.

you at the same time. As soon as he associates the word "come" with the action of moving toward you, pull only when he does not respond immediately. As he starts to come, move back to make him learn that he must come from a distance, as well as when he is close to you. Soon you may be able to practice without a leash, but if he is slow to come or notably disobedient, go to him and pull him toward you, repeating the command. Never scold a dog during this or any other exercise. Remember that the trick is that the puppy must want to come to you. Lavish your dog with praise each time he comes when called. An Ibizan Hound responds to praise and will reliably come when called only if he is taught he will be praised, no matter what he may have done, if he comes to you when called. For the independent dog or to ease this training, offer a treat when your Ibizan comes to you when called.

THE SIT COMMAND

As with most basic commands, your puppy will learn this one in just a few lessons. You can give the puppy two lessons a day on the sit command, but he will make just as much progress with one 15-minute lesson each day. Some trainers will advise you that you should not proceed to other commands until the previous one has been learned quite well. However, a bright, young pup is quite capable of handling more than one command per lesson and certainly per day. Indeed, as time progresses, you will be going through each command as a matter of routine before a new one is attempted. This is so the puppy always starts as well as ends a lesson on a high note, having successfully completed something.

Call the puppy to you and praise him. Place one hand on his hindquarters and the other under his upper chest. Say, "Sit" in a pleasant (never harsh) voice. At the same time, push down his rear end and push up under his chest. Now lavish praise on the puppy and give him a treat. Repeat this a few times, and your pet will get the idea. Once the puppy is in the sit position, you will release your hands. At first he will tend to get up, so immediately repeat the exercise. The lesson will end when the pup is in the sit position. When the puppy understands the command and does it right away, you can slowly move backward so that you are a few feet away from him. If he attempts to come to you, simply place him back in the original position and start again. Do not attempt to keep the pup in the sit position for too long. At this age, even a few seconds is a long while, and you do not want him to get bored with lessons before he has even begun them.

THE HEEL COMMAND

All dogs should be able to walk nicely on a leash with their owners without being involved in a tug-of-war. The heel command will follow leash training. Heel training is best done where you have a wall to one side of you. This will restrict the puppy's lateral movements so that you only have to contend with forward and backward situations. A fence is an alternative, or you can do the lesson in the garage. Again, it is better to do the lesson in private, not on a public sidewalk where there will be many distractions.

With a young puppy, there will be no need to use a choke collar, because you can be just as effective with a regular one. The leash should be of good length, certainly not too short. You can adjust the space between you, the puppy, and the wall, so that your pet has only a small amount of room to move sideways.

This being so, he will either hang back or pull ahead; the latter is the more desirable state as it indicates a bold pup that is not frightened of you.

With the puppy on your left side, hold the leash in your right hand and pass it through your left. As the puppy moves ahead and strains on the leash, give the leash a quick jerk backward with your left hand at the same time saying, "Heel." Be sure not to be too harsh. The jerk should stop your pup's forward motion but should not hurt him. The position you want the pup to be in is such that his chest is level with or just behind an imaginary line from your knee. When the puppy is in this position, praise him and begin walking again, and the whole exercise will be repeated. Once the puppy begins to get the message, you can use your left hand to pat the side of your leg.

It is useful to suddenly do an about-turn when the pup understands the basics. The puppy will now be behind you, so you can pat your knee and say "Heel." As soon as the pup is in the correct position, give him lots of praise. The puppy will now begin to associate

The heel exercise teaches your dog to walk beside you without pulling, which will make your daily outings together more enjoyable.

certain words with certain actions. Whenever he is not in the heel position, he will experience displeasure as you jerk the leash, but when he comes alongside you, he will receive praise. Given these two options, he will always prefer the latter, assuming he has no other reason to fear you, which would then create a di-lemma in his mind.

Once the dog has learned the lesson well, you can adjust your pace from a slow walk to a quick one, and the puppy will begin to adjust to your movements. The slow walk is always the more difficult for most pup-pies, as they are usually anxious to be on the move.

If you have no wall to walk against, things will be a little more difficult because the pup will tend to wander to his left. This means you need to give lateral jerks as well as bring the pup to your side. End the lesson when the pup is walking nicely beside you. Begin the lesson with a few sit commands, which he under-stands by now, so that you're starting with success and praise. If your puppy is nervous on the leash, you should never drag him to your side as you may see so many other people do. If the pup sits down, call him to your side and give lots of praise. The pup must always come to you because he wants to. If he is dragged to your side, he will see you doing the dragging—a big negative. When he races ahead, he does not see you jerk the leash, so all he knows is that something restricted his movement. Once he is in the given position, give him lots of praise. This is using canine psychology to your advantage.

Always keep in mind that if a dog must be disci-plined, he must not associate the discipline with you. This is not possible in all matters, but where it is, this is definitely preferred.

THE STAY COMMAND

This command follows from the sit and may be one of the more difficult commands for your active, inquisi-tive Ibizan Hound to master. Face the puppy and say, "Sit." Now step backward, and as you do, say, "Stay." Let the pup remain in the position for only a few seconds before calling him to you and giving lots of praise. Repeat this again, but step further back. You do not need to shout at the puppy. Your pet is not deaf; in fact, his hearing is far better than yours is. Speak just loudly enough for the pup to hear, yet use a firm voice. You can stretch the word to form a "Sta-a-a-y." If the pup gets up and comes to you, simply lift him up,

Aside from having very practical uses, the stay command teaches your dog self-control. He should be able to remain in position until you release him, as this obedient Ibizan demonstrates with a down/stay.

place him back in the original position, and start again. As the pup comes to understand the command, you can move further and further back.

The next test is to walk away after placing the pup. This will mean that your back is to him, which will tempt him to follow you. Keep an eye over your shoulder, and the minute the pup starts to move, turn around. In a sterner voice say either, "Sit" or "Stay." If the pup has gotten quite close to you, return him to the original position.

As the weeks go by, you can increase the length of time the dog is left in the stay position, but two to three minutes is quite long enough for a puppy. If your puppy drops into a lying position and is clearly more comfortable, there is nothing wrong with this. Like- wise, your pup will want to face the direction in which you walked off. Some trainers will prefer that the dog face the direction he was placed in, regardless of whether or not you move off on his blind side.

THE DOWN COMMAND

From the puppy's viewpoint, the down command can be one of the more difficult ones to accept, because the position is one taken up by a submissive dog in a wild pack situation. A timid dog will roll over, which is a natural gesture of submission. A bolder pup will want to get up and might back off, not feeling as if he should have to submit to this command. He will feel that he is under attack from you and about to be punished, which is what the position would be in his natural environment. Once he understands this is not the case, he will accept this unnatural position without any problem.

You may notice that some dogs will sit very quickly but will respond to the down command more slowly. It is their way of saying that they will obey the command, but under protest!

There are two ways to teach this command. One is more intimidating than the other, but it is up to you to decide which one works best for you and your Ibizan Hound. The first method is to stand in front of your puppy and bring him to the sit position, with his collar and leash on. Pass the leash under your left foot, so that when you pull on it, the result is that the pup's neck is slowly forced downward. With your free left hand, push the pup's shoulders down while at the same time saying, "Down." This is when a bold pup will instantly try to back off and wriggle in full protest. Hold the pup firmly by the shoulders, so that he stays in the position for a second or two then tell him what a good dog he is and give him lots of praise. If you offer your pup a treat while he is in the down position, he will relax and immediately associate a positive reward with this command. Repeat this only a few times in a lesson, otherwise the puppy will get bored and upset over this command. End with an easy command that brings back the pup's confidence.

The second method is to stand in front of the pup and then tell him to sit. Now kneel down, which is immediately far less intimidating to the puppy than to have you towering above him. Take each of his front legs and pull them forward, at the same time saying, "Down." Release the legs and quickly apply light pressure on the shoulders with your left hand. Then quickly say, "Good boy" and give lots of praise. Offer a treat as a reward. Repeat two or three times only. The pup will learn over a few lessons. Remember that this is a very submissive act on the pup's behalf, so there is no need to rush matters.

RECALL TO HEEL COMMAND

When your puppy is coming to the heel position from an off-leash situation (for example, if he has been running free), he should do this in the correct manner. He should pass behind you, take up his position, and then sit. To teach this command, have the pup in front of you in the sit position with his collar and leash on. Hold the leash in your right hand. Give him the command to heel and pat your left knee. As the pup starts to move forward, use your right hand to guide him behind you. If you need to, you can hold his collar and walk him around the back of you to the desired position. You will need to repeat this a few times until he understands what is wanted.

When he has done this a number of times, and you are sure that he will come to you when called, you can try it without the collar and leash. If the pup comes up toward your left side, bring him to the sit position in front of you, hold his collar, and walk him around the back of you. He will eventually understand and automatically pass around your back each time. If the dog is already behind you when you recall him, then he should automatically come to your left side, which you will be patting with your hand.

THE NO COMMAND

This is a command that must be obeyed every time without fail. There are no halfway stages; he must be 100 percent reliable. Most delinquent dogs have never been taught this command, including the jumpers, the barkers, and the biters. If your puppy were to approach a poisonous snake or any other potential danger, the no command, coupled with the recall, could save his life. You do not need to give a specific lesson for this command because it will crop up time and again in day-to-day life.

Be firm and consistent when teaching your Ibizan the no command. It could save his life someday and can help curb common behavior problems, like jumping up.

If the puppy is chewing a slipper, you should approach the pup, take hold of the slipper, and say, "No!" in a stern voice. If he jumps onto the furniture, lift him off, say, "No," and place him gently on the floor. You must be consistent in the use of the command and apply it every time he is doing something you do not want him to do.

Never allow your Ibizan pup to step out of the front door to your home or jump out of your car until you give him the command, "OK." If he does leave without your approval, say "No!" in a stern voice and place him back into the house or car. Do not allow him to step out of the door until he hears your command. Dogs are usually excited when they leave home, and this simple step can save your pup from excitedly running onto a busy street full of traffic.

SOCIALIZATION

When your Ibizan Hound puppy can walk nicely on a leash and has had his series of puppy shots, it is important to socialize him. Take him to public places, such as parks, often and allow him to become familiar with new sights, sounds, and people. This is an important step in the development of your puppy. Omitting the socialization of an Ibizan Hound puppy may result in a shy adult that is not comfortable around new people or situations.

The time invested in training will benefit both dog and owner for a lifetime.

SHOWING YOUR IBIZAN HOUND

The Ibizan is capable of being an impressive presence in the show ring. When competing in conformation events, he will be judged on how closely he resembles the standard of the breed.

Showing your Ibizan Hound can be a fun and rewarding experience for you and your dog. From the conformation ring to obedience, agility, lure coursing, or tracking, the versatile Ibizan can do it all. There are many things to consider before choosing an event to participate in. First, you must decide on your area of interest. Two important factors affecting this decision will probably be time and money. Time is an important

element because some events require long hours of training to ensure success. Expenses can differ with each event and costs to compete can run from a few dollars to several hundred dollars. Research your area of interest before making an investment.

CONFORMATION SHOWS

The thought of showing one's own dog in the conformation ring often makes the beginner nervous. To many people, dog shows have a certain mystique. The outdated image of high society and pampered pooches parading around the ring still exists in the minds of many people. Campaigning a top show dog can cost tens of thousands of dollars each year, and many kennels are designed specifically to produce champion show dogs. However, most show dogs, even some of the best champions, are simply much loved pets that are shown several times a year by their owners.

In conformation showing, you will be competing against other Ibizan Hounds, all of which are compared to the breed's standard of excellence by a judge. This breed standard gives a detailed description of the correct conformation, movement, temperament, and other qualities of the Ibizan Hound and is adopted by the kennel club that your dog is registered with, such as the American Kennel Club in the US or The Kennel Club in England. The judge examines each dog and chooses his or her winners based on how well the dogs conform to their breed standard. One dog from each breed is chosen for further competition against dogs of other breeds.

If you have never shown a dog before, an Ibizan Hound is an excellent breed to begin with because of his short coat and the ease of grooming. A simple bath, brushing, ear cleaning, and nail trim, and your dog is ready to enter the ring, unlike some of the coated breeds whose show preparation may take hours of professional grooming.

The manner in which your Ibizan Hound is presented to the judge can make a considerable difference in both your dog's appearance and the judge's impression of him. Any dog that is poorly handled in the ring will simply not look his best. Remember that this is a dog *show!* You and your Ibizan Hound must learn to do just that.

The best place to start is at a handling class. These classes are usually held about once a week. There,

Showing your Ibizan Hound can be a fun and rewarding experience for you and your dog. Am/Can. Ch. Bramblewood Husn Sharib Hawa and his owner, Carol Kaufman.

you and your dog will be with other owners and their dogs in a situation very similar to a real dog show. An instructor will act as the judge, examining your dog and instructing you to move your dog around the ring. Your Ibizan will become accustomed to unfamiliar surroundings, dogs, people, and actual ring procedure. Your instructor will give you tips on how to properly present your Ibizan Hound in the ring in order to make him look his best.

The perfect dog does not exist—every dog has his good features and his faults. Handlers are paid to make their client's dogs look great. A professional handler knows how to show off a dog's best features and cover up his faults. Good handlers are true professionals and worth every penny that they charge.

Novice exhibitors sometimes feel intimidated about showing against a professional handler. Remember

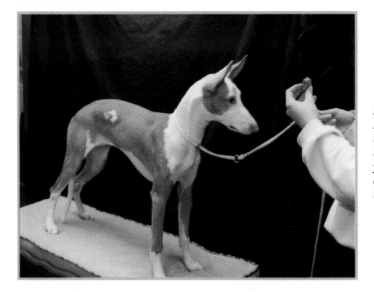

Five-month-old Ahram's High Hopes For Re is being trained to free-stack. Using bait, you can slowly coax your dog forward a step at a time until his feet are in the correct show stance.

that every handler started out as a beginner, just like you. After you have been in the ring a few times you will learn to relax and really enjoy the teamwork between you and your hound. Perhaps your dog has exceptionally good shoulder angulation or a very nice head. Be confident in your dog's good points and show off his best features to the judge. The following tips will help you in the ring.

The Ibizan Hound has moderate angulation. One of the most common mistakes made when showing this breed is to stretch the rear legs back too far while stacking the dog. (Stacking means to place your dog into a show stance, evenly positioning his legs in a manner that allows the judge to examine him and see his structure.) When stacking your hound, his rear pasterns (the part of the leg from hock to foot) should appear to be vertical when viewed from the side.

To really show off your Ibizan Hound, train him to free-stack. Stand in front of your dog with a piece of bait in your hand. (Bait is a show term for your dog's favorite food, such as bits of cooked liver.) As he watches you intently, use the bait to slowly coax him forward a step at a time until each of his feet are in the proper position. It will probably take many training sessions to master free-stacking. When your dog is in the correct position, softly toss rather than hand him little bits of the bait, which will encourage him to keep his ears erect. The goal of free-stacking is to have your hound learn to stand in a proper show stance with his ears up and an alert expression.

When moving an Ibizan Hound directly away from and directly toward the judge, keep his pace at a slow trot with a fairly loose lead. This will allow him to move at a natural hunting gait that will reveal his soundest (most correct) movement. Move in a straight line and allow your dog to do the same. When showing the judge your dog's side movement, move him at a brisk trot. The judge will be looking for smooth, flowing movement. This pace should be brisk but not excessive. The Ibizan is not built to have a natural stride that is as far-reaching as most other sighthound breeds, so if you move your dog at too fast a pace, his action will appear to be sloppy.

Every dog will not possess all of the qualities necessary to become a champion show dog. If you wish to pursue conformation showing, have your Ibizan Hound's breeder evaluate your dog when he is grown. If his attributes do not fall into the conformation show dog category, don't worry. He will probably excel in other areas, as the Ibizan is a very versatile breed. Always remember that whether show dog or pet, every dog deserves a great home with lots of love.

OBEDIENCE

Obedience is an event in which your dog is judged and awarded points based on how well he performs set exercises according to your directions. Obedience clubs offer training classes that are a valuable aid in preparing your dog for the obedience ring. There are several levels of achievement that are offered in obedience, and your dog will earn titles when he completes the requirements for each level. Many years of training are usually required to earn the higher titles of achievement.

Obedience trainers differ in their methods of training. The Ibizan Hound has a more sensitive nature than many other dog breeds. He wants to please his owner and trains well with a lot of praise, encouragement, and treats. Harsh training methods should never be used on this breed, as they will cause your Ibizan to become afraid of you. A fearful Ibizan Hound will never be reliable in his response to your commands. If your Ibizan Hound does not trust and respect you, he will react with sighthound aloofness, refusing to respond consistently or at times simply ignoring your commands. It will take many weeks to undo the damage done in just one harsh training session. Make sure that your obedience trainer understands and is willing to work with the unique personality of a sighthound.

AGILITY

If you like a fast-paced, fun sport where dog and handler must work closely together as a team, agility may be the event for you. The Ibizan Hound excels in the speed, agility, and jumping ability necessary for this event.

Agility originated in England and is rapidly gaining in popularity in many countries throughout the world. The rules may vary, as there are different governing associations that sanction agility trials. However, the goal is the same—to guide your dog over, around, and through the required obstacles in the shortest amount of time. Downed jumps or errors in performance count as faults. Dogs that are able to perform within the required time and fault limits obtain a leg (qualifying score) toward the completion of a title. There are many different titles that may be earned, and it can take many years of training to earn some of the more advanced ones.

The equipment used at an agility trial is required to conform to exact specifications. The expense of making and maintaining such equipment, along with the amount of room needed for training, is prohibitive to the individual. Agility clubs offer training classes where all of the necessary equipment is available for your use. The purpose of the class is to train you, as well as your Ibizan. At a training class, a qualified instructor can show you how to train your dog with the methods that are the safest and obtain the best results.

An agility dog is a true athlete. Do not push your dog, especially a young dog, too quickly or serious injury can result. Training should always remain a fun and positive experience, with lots of encouragement, praise, and treats for your Ibizan.

LURE COURSING

The Ibizan Hound's natural speed and stamina make this breed shine on the coursing field. Lure coursing consists of the attachment of an artificial lure to a string, in place of live game. This string is laid out in a specific pattern (called a course) over a large area. With the aid of a motor, it travels through pulleys at fast speeds. Hounds are released, usually three at a time, to chase the lure. The dogs are scored not only on their speed, but also on how intently they chase after the lure. Thousands of years of hunting have fine-tuned the Ibizan Hound for this sport.

Ibizans love lure coursing, because their inherent need to run and chase is fulfilled. Unlike obedience or agility, lure coursing is a sport where the Ibizan Hound uses his natural athletic ability and keen hunting instincts without the guidance of a human. The chance to run free in a seemingly wild situation is fun and exciting to the Ibizan.

Lure coursing clubs exist in many areas. These clubs offer practice sessions where your dog can become familiar with and excited about the sport. They will also sponsor lure coursing trials where your dog can earn points toward a coursing title. There are varying levels of achievement that can be attained in lure coursing. As there are different governing organizations that sanction trials and award titles for this event, rules and regulations for each organization vary somewhat.

There are other areas that might be of interest to you and your Ibizan Hound, such as tracking or retrieving. Be sure to attend the type of events that spark your interest. Talk to exhibitors about the sport. They can be of great help in guiding you in the right direction.

Many years of training are usually required to earn the higher titles of achievement. Best in Show winner Ch. Cesare's Flying First Class and owner/handler Leslie Lucas.

YOUR HEALTHY IBIZAN HOUND

Most Ibizan Hounds live a long and healthy life. Lifespans of 13 to 15 years are quite common in this breed; however, there are a few problems that may affect your Ibizan and you should be aware of what to watch for.

Dogs, like all other animals, are capable of contracting problems and diseases that, in most cases, are easily avoided by sound husbandry. This means that well-bred and well-cared-for animals are less prone to developing diseases and problems than are carelessly bred and neglected animals. Your knowledge of how to avoid problems is far more valuable than all of the books and advice on how to cure them. Respectively, the only person you should listen to about treatment is your vet. Veterinarians don't have all the answers, but at least they are trained to analyze and treat illnesses and are aware of the full implications of various treatments. This does not mean a few old remedies aren't good standbys when all else fails, but in most cases, modern science provides the best treatments for disease. Remember that many problems can be easily treated when caught early. At the first sign of a potential problem, always consult your veterinarian as soon as possible. An owner's neglect should never be the cause of a dog's suffering or untimely death.

Opposite: As a responsible Ibizan Hound owner, you should have an understanding of the medical problems that affect the breed.

PHYSICAL EXAMS

Your puppy should receive regular physical examinations or check-ups. These come in two forms—one is obviously performed by your vet and the other is a

Healthy teeth and gums are important to the well-being of your Ibizan. Check and brush his teeth regularly.

day-to-day procedure that should be done by you. Apart from the fact that the exam will highlight any problem at an early stage, it is an excellent way of socializing the pup to being handled.

To do the physical exam yourself, start at the head and work your way around the body. You are looking for any sign of lesions or any indication of parasites on the pup. The most common parasites are fleas and ticks.

HEALTHY TEETH AND GUMS

Chewing is instinctual. Puppies chew so that their teeth and jaws grow strong and healthy as they develop. As the permanent teeth begin to emerge, it is painful and annoying to the puppy, and puppy owners must recognize that their new charges need something safe upon which to chew. Unfortunately, once the puppy's permanent teeth have emerged and settled solidly into the jaw, the chewing instinct does not fade. Adult dogs instinctively need to clean their teeth, massage their gums, and exercise their jaws through chewing.

It is necessary for your dog to have clean teeth. You should take your dog to the veterinarian at least once a year to have his teeth cleaned and to have his mouth examined for any sign of oral disease. Although dogs do not get cavities in the same way humans do, dogs' teeth accumulate tartar more quickly than human's teeth do. Veterinarians recommend brushing your dog's teeth daily, but with our busy schedules, who can find time to do this on a daily basis? The accumulation of tartar and plaque on our dog's teeth, when not removed, can cause irritation, eventually erode the enamel, and finally destroy the teeth. Advanced cases, while destroying the teeth, bring on gingivitis and periodontitis, two very serious conditions that can affect the dog's internal organs as well—to say nothing about bad breath!

Because everyone can't brush their dog's teeth daily or get to the veterinarian often enough for him to scale the dog's teeth, providing the dog with something safe to chew on will help maintain oral hygiene. Chew devices from Nylabone® keep dogs' teeth clean, but they also provide an excellent resource for entertainment and relief of doggie tensions. Nylabone® products give your dog something to do for an hour or two every day, and during that hour or two your dog will be taking an active part in keeping his teeth and gums healthy without

Nylabone® is the only plastic dog bone made of 100% virgin nylon, specially processed to create a tough, durable, completely safe bone.

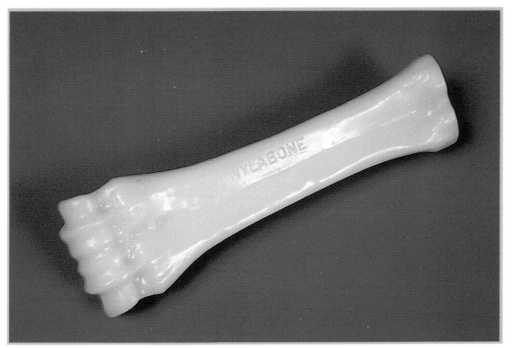

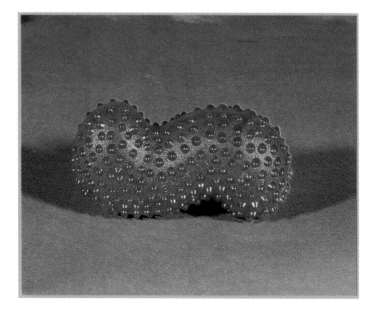

The Hercules ® by Nylabone® has raised dental tips that help fight plaque on your Ibizan's teeth.

even realizing it. That's invaluable to your dog and valuable to you.

FIGHTING FLEAS

Ibizan Hounds can have allergic reactions to fleas, so it is imperative to keep your dog's quarters free from these pests.

Fleas are very mobile and may be red, black, or brown in color. The adults suck the blood of the host, while the larvae feed on the feces of the adults, which is rich in blood. Flea "dirt" may be seen on the pup as very tiny clusters of blackish specks that look like freshly ground pepper. The eggs of fleas may be laid on the dog, though they are more commonly laid off the host in a favorable place such as the bedding. They normally hatch in 4 to 21 days, depending on the temperature, but they can survive for up to 18 months if temperature conditions are not favorable. The larvae are maggot-like and molt a couple of times before forming pupae, which can survive long periods until the temperature or the vibration of a nearby host causes them to emerge. When they find a host, they jump on and the cycle begins again.

There are a number of effective treatments available that you should discuss with your veterinarian, then follow all the instructions for the one that you choose. Any treatment will involve a product for your puppy or dog and one for the environment and will require diligence on your part to treat all areas and thoroughly clean your home and yard until the infestation is eradicated.

THE TROUBLE WITH TICKS

Ticks are arthropods of the spider family, which means they have eight legs (though the larvae have six). They bury their head parts into the host and gorge on its blood. They are easily seen as small, grain-like creatures sticking out from the skin. They are often picked up when dogs play in fields but may also arrive in your yard via wild animals such as birds or stray animals such as cats and dogs. Some ticks are species specific, and others are more adaptable and will host on many species. The most troublesome type of tick is the deer tick, which spreads the deadly Lyme disease that can cripple a dog (or a person). Deer ticks are tiny and very hard to detect. Often, by the time they're big enough to be noticed, they've been feeding on the dog for a few days, which is long enough to do their damage. Lyme disease was named for the area of the United States in which it was first detected, Lyme, Connecticut, but has now been diagnosed in almost all parts of the US. Your veterinarian can advise you of the danger to your dog in your area and may suggest your dog be vaccinated for Lyme disease. Always go over your dog with a fine-toothed flea comb when you come in from walking through any area that may harbor deer ticks, and if your dog is acting unusually sluggish or sore, seek veterinary advice.

Attempts to pull a tick free will invariably leave the head part in the dog, where it will die and cause an infected wound or abscess. The best way to remove ticks is to dab a strong saline solution, iodine, or

The cat flea is the most common flea of dogs. It starts feeding soon after it makes contact with the dog.

The deer tick is the most common carrier of Lyme disease. Photo courtesy of Virbac Laboratories, Inc., Fort Worth, Texas.

alcohol on them. This will numb them, causing them to loosen their hold, at which time they can be removed with forceps. The wound can then be cleaned and covered with an antiseptic ointment. If ticks are common in your area, consult with your vet for a suitable pesticide to be used in kennels, on bedding, and on the puppy or dog.

INSECTS AND OTHER DANGERS

There are many biting insects that can cause discomfort to a dog, such as mosquitoes. The males of these species can transmit several diseases. Many Ibizan Hounds are unusually sensitive to insect bites. Some dogs may even go into shock from something as seemingly minor as a wasp sting. Often, the skin in the area involved will turn pink and the dog will become very uncomfortable and agitated. It is important to immediately take your dog to the vet if you suspect he is having serious trouble associated with an insect bite.

While walking outside, a dog can easily get a grass seed or thorn lodged between his pads. These may go unnoticed until an abscess forms. This is where your daily check of the puppy or dog will do a world of good. If your pet has been playing in long grass or places where there may be thorns, pine needles, wild animals, or parasites, the check-up is a wise precaution.

SKIN DISORDERS

Apart from problems associated with lesions created by biting pests, a dog may develop a number of other skin disorders. Examples are ringworm, mange,

Opposite: There are many parasites, like fleas and ticks, that your dog can encounter when playing outside. Be sure to check your Ibizan's coat thoroughly after he comes in from the outdoors.

and eczema. Ringworm is not caused by a worm but is a fungal infection. It manifests itself as a sore-looking bald circle. If your dog should have any form of bald patches, let your veterinarian check him over; a microscopic examination can confirm the condition. Many old remedies for ringworm exist, such as iodine, carbolic acid, formalin, and other tinctures, but modern drugs are superior.

Fungal infections can be very difficult to treat and even more difficult to eradicate because of the spores. These can withstand most treatments other than burning. Bedding should be incinerated or properly discarded once the condition has been confirmed.

Mange is a general term that can be applied to many skin conditions where the hair falls out and a flaky crust develops and falls away. Often, dogs will scratch themselves, and this invariably is worse than the original condition, for it opens lesions that are then subject to viral, fungal, or parasitic attack. The cause of the problem can be various species of mites. These either live on skin debris and the hair follicles, which they destroy, or they bury themselves just beneath the skin and feed on the tissue. Applying general

It cannot be overstressed that it is not wise to attempt to diagnose an internal disorder without the advice of a veterinarian.

remedies from pet stores is not recommended because it is essential to identify the type of mange before a specific treatment is effective.

Eczema is another non-specific term applied to many skin disorders. The condition can be brought about in many ways. Sunburn, chemicals, allergies to foods, drugs, pollens, and even stress can all produce a deterioration of the skin and coat. Given the range of causal factors, treatment can be difficult because the problem is one of identification. It is a case of taking each possibility at a time and trying to correctly diagnose the matter. If the cause is of a dietary nature, then you must remove one item at a time in order to find out if the dog is allergic to a given food. It could, of course, be the lack of a nutrient that is the problem, so if the condition persists, you should consult your veterinarian.

Some Ibizans seem particularly prone to skin rashes. Allergic reactions to topical treatments such as scented dog shampoos and even flea and tick collars and dips have been reported. Most dogs will not experience any problems, but be wary when using any new products.

INTERNAL DISORDERS

It cannot be overstressed that it is very foolish to attempt to diagnose an internal disorder without the advice of a veterinarian. For example, take a relatively common problem such as diarrhea. It might be caused by nothing more serious than the dog hogging a lot of food or eating something that he has never previously eaten. Conversely, it could be the first indication of a potentially fatal disease. It's up to your veterinarian to make the correct diagnosis.

The following symptoms, especially if they accompany each other or are progressively added to earlier symptoms, mean you should visit the veterinarian right away:

Continual Vomiting

All dogs vomit from time to time, and this is not necessarily a sign of illness. They will eat grass to induce vomiting. It is a natural cleansing process common to many omnivores. However, continued vomiting is a clear sign of a problem. It may be due to a blockage in the dog's intestinal tract, it may be induced by worms, or it could be due to any number of diseases.

Make an appointment with the vet if your Ibizan's behavior changes. For example, a loss of interest in food, prolonged listlessness, or crying can indicate a health problem.

Diarrhea

This, too, may be nothing more than a temporary condition due to many factors. Even a change of home can induce diarrhea because this often stresses the dog and invariably there is some change in the diet. If it persists more than 48 hours, then something is amiss. If blood is seen in the feces, waste no time at all in taking the dog to the vet.

Running Eyes or Nose

A pup might have a chill, and this will cause the eyes and nose to weep. Again, this should quickly clear up if the puppy is placed in a warm environment and away from any drafts. If it does not, especially if a mucous discharge is seen, then the dog has an illness that must be diagnosed.

Coughing

Prolonged coughing is a sign of a problem, usually of a respiratory nature. If the dog has difficulty breathing or makes a wheezing sound when breathing, then something is wrong.

Crying

Crying while trying to defecate might only be a minor problem due to the hard state of the feces, but it could be more serious, especially if the dog cries when urinating. Obviously, if you do not handle a puppy with care, he might yelp. However, if he cries even when lifted gently or if the adult dog whimpers when he moves, then he has an internal problem that becomes apparent when pressure is applied to a given area of the body. Clearly, this must be diagnosed.

Refuses Food

Generally, puppies and dogs are greedy creatures when it comes to feeding times. Some might be fussier, but none should refuse more than one meal. If they go for a number of hours without showing any interest in their food, then something is not as it should be.

General Listlessness

All dogs have off days when they do not seem their usual cheeky, mischievous selves. If this condition persists for more than two days, then there is little doubt that there is a problem. They may not show any of the signs listed, other than perhaps a reduced interest in their food. There are many diseases that can develop internally without displaying obvious signs. Blood, fecal, and other tests are needed in order to identify the disorder before it reaches an advanced state that may not be treatable.

WORMS

There are many species of worms, and a number of these live in the tissues of dogs and most other animals. Many create no problem at all, so you are not

Roundworms are spaghetti-like worms that cause a pot-bellied appearance and dull coat, along with more severe symptoms, such as dairrhea and vomiting. Photo courtesy of Merck AgVet.

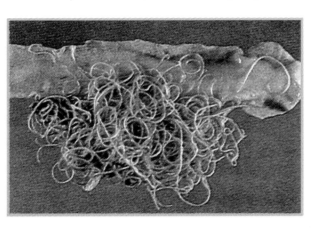

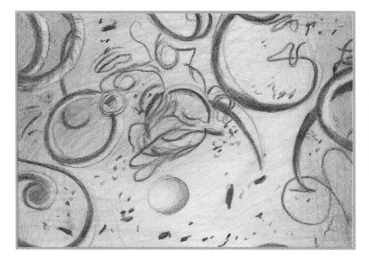

Whipworms are hard to find unless you strain your dog's feces, and this is best left to your veterinarian. Pictured here are adult whipworms.

even aware they exist. Others can be tolerated in small levels but become a major problem if they number more than a few. The most common types seen in dogs are roundworms and tapeworms. While roundworms are the greater problem, tapeworms require an intermediate host and so are more easily eradicated.

Roundworms of the species *Toxocara canis* infest the dog. They may grow to a length of 8 inches (20 cm) and look like strings of spaghetti. The worms feed on the digesting food in the dog's intestines. In chronic cases, the dog will become pot-bellied, have diarrhea, and will vomit. Eventually, he will stop eating, after having passed through the stage when he always seems hungry. The worms lay eggs in the dog and these pass out in his feces. The dog then either ingests them or mice, rats, or beetles eat them. These may then be eaten by the dog, and the life cycle is complete.

Larval worms can migrate to the womb of a pregnant bitch or to her mammary glands, and this is how they pass to the puppy. The pregnant bitch can be wormed, which will help. The pups can and should be wormed when they are about two weeks old. Repeat the worming every 10 to 14 days, after which the parasites should be removed. Worms can be extremely dangerous to young puppies, so you should be sure the pup is wormed as a matter of routine.

Tapeworms can be seen as tiny, rice-like eggs sticking to the puppy's or dog's anus. They are less destructive but still undesirable. The eggs are eaten by mice, fleas, rabbits, and other animals that serve as intermediate hosts. They develop into a larval stage, and the dog must eat the host in order to complete the chain. Your vet will supply a suitable remedy if tapeworms are seen or suspected. There are other worms such as hookworms and whipworms that are also blood suckers. They will make a dog anemic, and blood might be seen in the feces, which can be examined by the vet to confirm their presence. Cleanliness in all matters is the best preventive measure for all worms.

Heartworm infestation in dogs is passed by mosquitoes but can be prevented by a monthly (or daily) treatment that is given orally. Talk to your vet about the risk of heartworm in your area.

BLOAT (GASTRIC DILATATION)

Bloat has proved to be fatal in many dogs, especially large and deep-chested breeds; however, any dog can get bloat. The Ibizan Hound is no exception, and although not an extremely common problem, Ibizans have died from this malady.

Bloat is caused by swallowing air during exercise, gulping food or water, or performing a strenuous task. As many believe, it is not the result of flatulence. The stomach of the affected dog twists, disallowing food and blood flow and resulting in harmful toxins being released into the bloodstream. Death can easily follow if the condition goes undetected. As the name implies, symptoms may include a bloated look to the dog's stomach area. The dog may also exhibit signs of being uncomfortable.

The best preventative measure is not to feed large meals or exercise your puppy or dog immediately after he has eaten. Veterinarians recommend feeding three smaller meals per day in an elevated feeding rack, adding water to dry food to prevent gulping, and not offering water during mealtimes.

VACCINATIONS

Every puppy, purebred or mixed breed, should be vaccinated against the major canine diseases. These are distemper, leptospirosis, hepatitis, coronavirus, and canine parvovirus. Your puppy should have received a temporary vaccination against these diseases before you purchased him, but ask the breeder to be sure. Additionally, there is an intranasal spray available that provides protection against canine cough.

The age at which vaccinations are given can vary, but most Ibizan Hound breeders give the first puppy shots at around six weeks of age. Being a larger breed of dog that grows quickly, Ibizan Hound puppies are usually introduced to solid foods while still nursing from their mothers at around four weeks of age and weaned earlier than many smaller breeds. Thus, antibodies received from the puppy's mother, via her milk, may wane by six weeks of age. Your veterinarian is your best source of advice on the proper timing of your puppy's first shots.

The puppy's immune system works on the basis that the white blood cells engulf and render harmless the attacking bacteria; however, they must first recognize a potential enemy. Vaccines are either dead bacteria, or they are live, but in very small doses. Either type prompts the pup's defense system to attack them. When a large attack comes (if it does), the immune system recognizes it and massive numbers of lymphocytes (white blood corpuscles) are mobilized to counter the attack. However, the ability of the cells to recognize these dangerous viruses can diminish over a period of time. Therefore, it is useful to provide annual reminders about the nature of the enemy. This is done by means of booster injections that keep the immune system on its alert. Immuniza-

Rely on your veterinarian for the most effective vaccination schedule for your Ibizan Hound puppy.

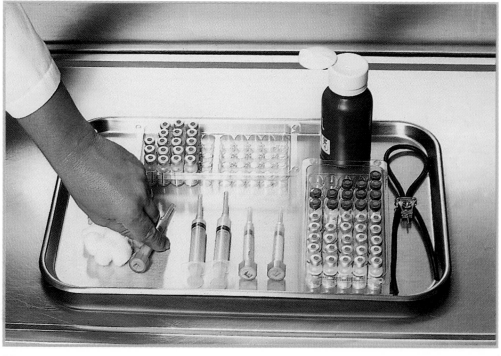

tion is not 100 percent guaranteed to be successful, but it is very close. Certainly, it is better than giving the puppy no protection.

Dogs are subject to other viral attacks and if these are of a high-risk factor in your area, then your vet will suggest you have the puppy vaccinated against these as well.

Your puppy or dog should also be vaccinated against the deadly rabies virus. In fact, in many places it is illegal for your dog not to be vaccinated. This is to protect your dog, your family, and the rest of the animal population from this deadly virus that infects the nervous system and causes dementia and death. In most places, this must be given by a veterinarian, and proof of such will usually be needed to obtain a license for you dog. Check the local ordinances in your area.

ANESTHESIA

As with many sighthounds, some Ibizans have exhibited problems when administered anesthesia. Before any surgery requiring that your dog be given anesthesia, you should remind your veterinarian of the Ibizan's sensitivity in this area so that he or she can be sure to use the safest anesthesia for your sighthound.

AXONAL DYSTROPHY

This rare disorder, which affects young puppies by the time they are four to six months of age, causes an uncoordinated, stumbling movement. Although considered an inherited disorder, the number of dogs actually examined by a veterinary specialist and confirmed to have this problem are very few. Regardless, Ibizan Hound owners should be aware of this problem.

CANCER

Cancer is on the rise in both humans and dogs. It is important to check your Ibizan Hound regularly for any signs of lumps or changes in the skin. Run your hands slowly and carefully over his body, feeling for any lumps under the skin or growths that may be on the skin. Don't forget to check between your dog's toes. If you feel a lump, have your vet examine it as soon as possible. Some lumps are nothing to worry about; however, some innocent looking lumps may turn cancerous and the sooner that these are removed, the less chance that the disease will spread.

Spaying and neutering your pet is the best way to prevent cancers that form in the reproductive system. The best time to have these procedures performed is around six months of age, before your dog becomes sexually mature.

EYE DISORDERS

Juvenile cataracts and progressive retinal atrophy (PRA) affect many breeds of dog. Most Ibizan Hound breeders have their dog's eyes screened by a veterinary specialist for disorders, so eye problems remain almost unseen today in the breed. Juvenile cataracts affect young dogs and may or may not cause blindness. The onset of PRA can be anywhere from a few months to several years of age. Night blindness is one of the first symptoms, which progresses to total blindness over a period of time.

SEIZURES

Seizures occur in dogs and can be caused by a number of reasons. Some seizures may appear to be hereditary in nature, resembling epilepsy in EEG readings. These seizures can start in the first year of life, but more commonly start in the second year. There are a number of documented causes for seizures in dogs—vitamin deficiencies, hypocalcemia, intestinal parasites or obstructions, hyperthermia, tick paralysis, meningitis, and other causes. Seizures can be a particularly heartbreaking occurrence to an owner. Testing to find the true cause of a dog's seizures may not be carried out because such tests can sometimes be quite expensive. These tests, although costly, are an important tool for the breeder who is concerned that their breeding program remains free from problems. Treatment for seizures usually consists of drug therapy, which has varying results.

ACCIDENTS

All puppies will get their share of bumps and bruises due to the rather energetic way they play. These will usually heal themselves over a few days. Small cuts should be bathed with a suitable disinfectant and then smeared with an antiseptic ointment. If a cut looks more serious, then stem the flow of blood with a towel or makeshift tourniquet and rush the pup to the veterinarian. Never apply so much pressure to the wound that it might restrict the flow of blood to the limb.

In the case of burns, you should apply cold water or an ice pack to the surface. If the burn was due to a chemical, then this must be washed away with ample amounts of water. Apply petroleum jelly or any vegetable oil to the burn. Trim away the hair if need be. Wrap the dog in a blanket and rush him to the vet. The pup may go into shock, depending on the severity of the burn. This will result in a lowered blood pressure, which is dangerous and the reason the pup must receive immediate veterinary attention.

If a broken limb is suspected, then try to keep the animal as still as possible. Wrap your pup or dog in a blanket to restrict movement and get him to the

If your Ibizan sustains an injury from an accident or fall, acting quickly and appropriately can save his life. For example, it's a good idea to x-ray any dog hit by a car.

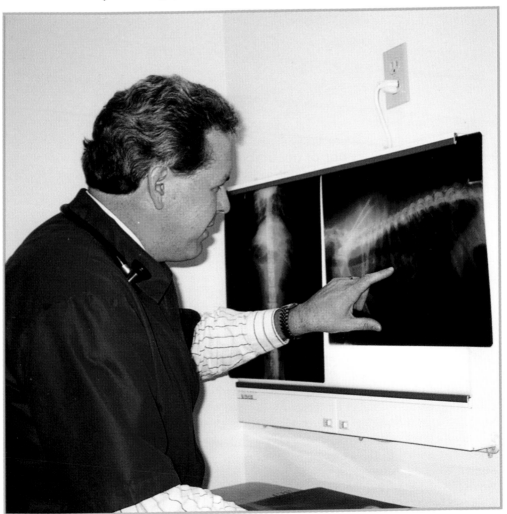

A daily checkup can help you to stay on top of your Ibizan's physical condition, as well as increase the communication between you and your pet.

veterinarian as soon as possible. Do not move the dog's head so it is tilting backward, as this might result in blood entering the lungs.

Do not let your pup jump up and down from heights, because it can cause considerable shock to the joints. Like all youngsters, puppies do not know when enough is enough, especially a rambunctious, agile Ibizan Hound puppy, so you must do all of their thinking for them.

Provided that you apply strict hygiene to all aspects of raising your puppy, and that you make daily checks on his physical state, you have done as much as you can to safeguard him during his most vulnerable period. Routine visits to your veterinarian are also recommended, especially while the puppy is under one year of age. The vet may notice something that did not seem important to you.

Opposite: Remember, regular physical examinations are tantamount to the health and long life of your dog. Am/Can. Ch. Serandida Iwazzu Al Iraaqi. Owner: Carol Kauffman.

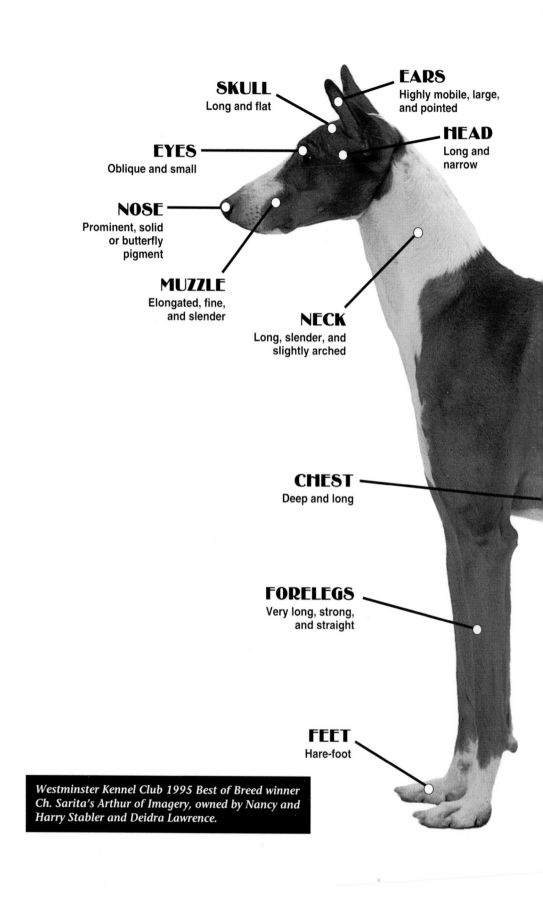

SKULL
Long and flat

EARS
Highly mobile, large,
and pointed

HEAD
Long and
narrow

EYES
Oblique and small

NOSE
Prominent, solid
or butterfly
pigment

MUZZLE
Elongated, fine,
and slender

NECK
Long, slender, and
slightly arched

CHEST
Deep and long

FORELEGS
Very long, strong,
and straight

FEET
Hare-foot

*Westminster Kennel Club 1995 Best of Breed winner
Ch. Sarita's Arthur of Imagery, owned by Nancy and
Harry Stabler and Deidra Lawrence.*